Praise for *Judaism: A Brief Guide to Faith*

In my thirty-five years of involvement in Christian-
book presents the most sensitive and comprehensive introduction to Judaism
I have ever read. Sharon Pace has written a positive presentation without
polemics, that is respectful and fair to all the diversity within modern
American Judaism: Orthodox, Conservative, Reform, Reconstructionist and
secularist points of view. It is a must-read for seminary students, priests,
women religious, religious educators, and all adult learners desiring a ready
guide to Jewish faith and practice.

—Richard C. Lux
Professor Emeritus in Scripture Studies
Sacred Heart School of Theology

This book is an invitation you will want to accept. Sharon Pace's concise
introduction acquaints the reader with central tenets of Jewish faith and the
practices that sustain it. The reader learns how these everyday practices, special ways of marking marriage, birth, and death, and the celebration of
Shabbat and religious holidays participate in God's creativity and help make
the world a dwelling place for God. *Judaism* breathes reverence, optimism,
and wisdom.

—Anathea E. Portier-Young
Associate Professor of Old Testament
Duke University Divinity School

Judaism is an open-source religion continually shaped and reshaped by Jews
across the millennia, and while there can be no single definitive expression of
the faith, Sharon Pace's *Judaism: A Brief Guide to Faith and Practice* is a solid
articulation of mainstream Judaism as most Jews encounter it. This book sets
forth the essential teachings and practices of Judaism and will be of benefit
to Jews seeking to know more about their faith, and Christians seeking to
know more about the faith of their Founder.

—Rabbi Rami Shapiro
Author of *Mount & Mountain*

Smyth & Helwys Publishing, Inc.
6316 Peake Road
Macon, Georgia 31210-3960
1-800-747-3016
©2012 by Sharon Pace
All rights reserved.
Printed in the United States of America.

The paper used in this publication meets the minimum requirements of
American National Standard for Information Sciences—
Permanence of Paper for Printed Library Materials.
ANSI Z39.48–1984. (alk. paper)

Library of Congress Cataloging-in-Publication Data

Pace, Sharon.
Judaism : a brief guide to faith and practice / by Sharon Pace.
p. cm.
ISBN 978-1-57312-644-1 (alk. paper)
1. Judaism. I. Title.
BM45.P25 2012
296--dc23

2012027750

JUDAISM

A Brief Guide to
Faith and Practice

Sharon Pace

ALSO BY SHARON PACE

Daniel (Smyth & Helwys Bible Commentary Series)

Old Testament Women (The Storyteller's Companion to the Bible)

The Women of Genesis: From Sarah to Potiphar's Wife

To Brian

Contents

Preface

The purpose of this book is to provide an introduction to the faith and practices of the Jewish people in a succinct and—I hope—interesting manner. Judaism's belief in the One God who is Creator of the Universe, the Redeemer of Israel and of all humanity, and the author of the torah (God's revelation) permeates all aspects of Judaism, from religious beliefs to life-cycle events to everyday behavior. What is it like to be born into the Jewish community? How does belief in the One God and a universal morality shape the way in which Jews see the world? How does one find meaning in life and the courage to endure suffering? How does one mark joy and forge community ties? By examining these details of Jewish life, one can see how Jews have defined themselves and their relationship to the Almighty, how they have identified tools for a righteous and purposeful existence, and how they hope to make the world a dwelling place for God. Moses told his people that torah was not across the sea, distant and impossible to find; rather, God's blueprint for living was close to their hearts. The sparks of the divine presence—God's holiness— permeate everyday lives. Jewish prayer, holidays, life-cycle events, holy texts, and traditions all mark times and seasons, enriching Jewish memory and life with incalculable meaning.

This book is designed for adult learners with little to no knowledge of Judaism. It would be appropriate for Christian study groups, for university students taking courses on Judaism or world religions, and for others looking for an overview of Jewish thought and life. It details Judaism's faith and traditions by examining belief, prayer, life-cycle practices, religious and secular holidays, and the attachment to Israel. It is my hope that this study will give the reader a view of Judaism through both my academic and my personal perspective—as a Jew who both teaches classes on Jewish thought in an academic context and whose own life is infused and enhanced by Jewish practice.

I would like to close with a word of appreciation to Keith Gammons and Leslie Andres. It is a joy for me to work with Smyth & Helwys.

Chapter 1

God: Creator, Redeemer, Revealer

"I am my beloved's and my beloved is mine." (Song 6:3)

In Jewish tradition, the fidelity that the beloved of King Solomon expresses in this verse symbolizes Israel's love for God. On one level of interpretation—the plain meaning—the speaker unabashedly proclaims her dedication to her soul mate. But on a deeper level, her declaration symbolizes the voice of the Jewish people calling to the Almighty. The children of Abraham and Sarah—attached to God ever since he offered an eternal promise for land and descendants, and bound by the covenant (the torah) forged at Sinai—call out to their Beloved, expressing love and intimacy. Judaism is the story of a relationship between God and Israel. Choice, passion, broken-heartedness, reconciliation, completeness in each other, and a shared vision characterize the unbreakable bond that exists between God and his people. In Jewish thought, each word of torah (teaching, instruction, law, [the Jewish] Bible) has incalculable meaning, endless value, and vast implications. This book invites the reader to explore the love story between the Almighty and his people—between God and Israel. There is an exalted purpose to this narrative: together, God and his people act as partners in making the world a dwelling place for the divine presence in which all people and all of creation are guided by divine providence.

"God saw everything that he had made, and indeed, it was very good" (Gen 1:31).[1] A world by design—a place of purpose and meaning, a place that is good—is the world in which humanity is placed. Judaism boldly proclaims that despite the human experience of brokenness, suffering, and futility, God created and continues to sustain a world in which no leaf ever falls without the expressed purpose of the Creator. To be sure, the beauty and power of nature pulls many people toward an acknowledgment of the Creator, as is seen in this psalm:

O LORD, our Sovereign,
  how majestic is your name in all the earth!
You have set your glory above the heavens . . . .
When I look at your heavens, the work of your fingers,
  the moon and the stars that you have established;
what are human beings that you are mindful of them,
  mortals that you care for them? (Ps 8:1-4)

The Creator of heaven and earth is the One God who has a relationship with humanity, giving all people a blueprint that can guide them throughout their lives.

Creator and Sustainer of the World

The way in which God created the world reflects the purpose of the divine plan. Let us consider the account of creation in seven days (Gen 1:1–2:4). Its structure is as follows:

Day 1: Light	Day 4: Luminaries and calendar
Day 2: Sky (or firmament), with waters above and waters below	Day 5: Creatures of the sky and sea
Day 3: Dry land	Day 6: Creatures of the land

Day 7: Shabbat

In Hebrew, the words "seven" and "Shabbat" come from the same root word meaning "completeness" or "wholeness." This is the central idea behind the seven-day creation schema in Jewish teaching. God created the world and everything in it with eternal guidance and care; all of creation is permeated with God's direction and supervision. This is reflected by the parallel structure of the first six days that culminate in the singular Sabbath (the seventh day) that, in contrast, has no counterpart.

What is the light created on the first day? It cannot be the sun, for that is created on the fourth day. The holy books of Judaism (the Mishnah, Talmud, and Midrashim) speak of these possibilities: perhaps it is the very light of God, associated with his goodness, that pervades the world; perhaps it is human consciousness or awareness—another gift that God gives to humanity; or perhaps it is a unique light that illumined the days of God's creation. Jewish tradition teaches that when God completed his creation, he saw that humanity was increasingly preoccupied with evil and violence; thus, he hid this special light for the righteous in the time to come—a time of an idealized future in which creation will be untainted by humanity's disobedience.[2] God concealed this light so that human evil would not annihilate the essential goodness of the world. This interpretation teaches that humans must work to discover righteousness in the world and that their quest will not be in vain, for "the light of the righteous rejoices" (Prov 13:9).

Though its interpretation is opaque, the *idea* of light is clearly associated with the goodness of God's design. The parallel to the creation of the first day is found on the fourth, when the individual luminaries were fashioned. The sun, moon, and stars not only serve as testimony to God's grandeur but also act as "signs and for seasons and for days and years" (Gen 1:14). In effect, they constitute a calendar. Calendars, to be sure, are essential for agriculture. Marking the times of planting and harvest, they help to sustain all human beings and all domesticated animals. Within Jewish life, in addition, the luminaries also designate sacred times and seasons. The Jewish calendar is determined by both the lunar and solar systems, and the difference between day and night is distinguished by the presence of stars. With this calendar, Jews mark the weekly day of rest (Shabbat) that is dedicated to the service of God, the religious festivals that occur once a year, and the beginning of each Hebrew month that is acknowledged with special blessings. These holy times are so essential to Israel and to God's relationship with the Jewish people that they are portrayed as foundational—they were established by God in the makeup of time itself.

On the second day, God created the sky (the firmament), separating the unruly waters above from the chaotic waters below. The idea of separation predominates in Jewish thinking because it is foundational for the idea of holiness. In Hebrew, to be holy means to be set apart—designated for a special purpose. With the creation of the sky, God brought order into the world that was previously "*tohu* and *bohu*"—marked by "formlessness and void" (Gen 1:2). The parallel to the second day is found in the fifth: the waters above and below the sky, that is, the heavens and the seas, were filled with life; God created the birds and all the sea creatures. Similarly, with the third day, we find separation with a purpose: God parted the seas, making the earth. On its parallel day, the sixth day, the earth is filled with the creatures of the land: insects, domestic and wild animals, and human beings (Gen 1:24-27).

Only the seventh day stands alone, without parallel. On this day, "God rested from all the work that he had done in creation" (Gen 2:3). In Judaism, this seventh day is hallowed as Shabbat. In God's divine plan, this designated day is essential. In contrast to other philosophical systems that define the value of the human beings by what they produce, Judaism asserts a very different concept: human beings *essentially* have meaning and purpose *apart from* anything they construct. All human beings are precious to God—men, women, young, old, abled, disabled—because all imitate God. And, on one day a week, Israel rests, replicating the act of the Creator, who also rested in time. What did God do on this day? God reflected on everything that he made, seeing that it was "very good" (Gen 1:31). And so, too, for Israel: on Shabbat, Jews draw closer to the divine presence, reflecting on God's blessings to each individual and to the world. On this hallowed day, they are reminded—from torah readings, prayer, ceremony, and community—how to make this world a better dwelling place for God, striving to be partners with the Almighty in creation.

In Jewish thought, God not only designed the heavens and earth to reflect their harmony and purposefulness but also created some things that are so essential that they warrant specific mention in the interpretive traditions of Judaism—in holy writings found outside of the Bible. These crucial entities are known as the things created by God even *before* the beginning of the world! By examining them, we can see some additional key Jewish ideas regarding God's role in creation. Before God formed the heavens and the earth, he created the following: repentance and torah, hell and heaven, the celestial temple and the divine throne, and the name of the messiah.[3] We now examine the significance of these concepts.

The creation of repentance and torah shows that, in the very fabric of human existence, people have the possibility of reconciliation with their Creator. A world without forgiveness from one's fellow human beings would be a terrible place indeed. How much more so would be a world without reconciliation with God! But with the creation of repentance, humans are blessed with the possibility of a constant relationship with the Almighty. By creating the torah, God constructed a world in which he purposefully and specifically guides human beings. What is torah? *Torah* refers to all of God's teaching, instruction, and law given to Moses on Mt. Sinai and passed on through each generation. Besides detailing the unique practices of Jewish life, the torah includes principles of morality and ethics intended for non-Jews as well. God instructs all humankind as a beloved teacher and commander, with specifics of what people must do to follow in his ways of righteousness, pleasantness, and truth (Prov 3:17).

With the creation of heaven and hell, God discloses that we live in a world of consequences, one in which the actions of human beings matter. God is the judge of all, rewarding justice and good deeds. The counterpoint is also true: God responds to injustice, punishing evildoers. The creation of the Throne of Glory shows that God did not make the world once in time only to abandon it. Rather, God keeps mindful watch over all that occurs, ruling as sovereign of the universe. Because God is king, morality and ethics remain constant. No human despot can usurp God's judgment of what is right and wrong; neither can ordinary people—even with all good intentions—make their laws or personal actions triumph over divine scrutiny. In addition, because God reigns, no creature exists on earth devoid of God's providence and care.

Why is the heavenly temple also an essential element of creation? The heavenly temple serves as a model for the earthy temple. With the temple (and its biblical precursor, the tabernacle or sanctuary), God established a special place to call home on earth. He tells Moses to proclaim to the Israelites, "And have them make me a sanctuary, so that I may dwell *among them*" (Exod 25:8). Jewish interpretation underscores that God did not say, "And have them make me a sanctuary so that I may dwell *in it.*" By emphasizing that God would dwell "among them" (i.e., among the people)—instead of highlighting that he would live "in it" (i.e., in the edifice)—the text prioritizes the importance of God's presence among the living community. Here we see that the idea of the sanctuary or temple transcends its physicality. The Jewish biblical commentator Don Isaac Abravanel (1437–1508) reflected,

> The Divine intention behind the construction of the Tabernacle [the sanctuary] was to combat the idea that God had forsaken the earth, and that his throne was in heaven and remote from humankind. . . . He commanded them to make a Tabernacle, as if to imply that He dwelt in their midst, that they should believe that God lived in their midst and His Providence was ever with them.[4]

It is extraordinary that God would dwell on earth, but even more so that he would dwell among human beings. This very world, with all its beauty and with all its conflict and suffering, can be a place for God.

Last in this list of the foundations of the divine creation, we find that God fashioned the name of the messiah. Judaism holds that the messiah— the anointed designate of God's choosing—is yet to come. Jews express their hope for his coming in daily prayer, awaiting the redemption of the world. The belief in the goodness of God's creation and the ultimate perfection of the world at the time of the final redemption is so essential that it finds expression in the foundations of God's creation.

Although the ways of the world wrench the human heart with their fractures and divisions, Judaism refuses to see God's creation as fundamentally broken. It may appear that competing realities vie for humanity's commitment and attention, but, in essence, all of creation comes from a loving God who is One. Thus, the watchword of Israel's faith is this: "Hear (Hebrew: *shema*), O Israel: The LORD is our God, the LORD alone" (Deut 6:4). No other reality competes with God; no idea or material thing demands unwavering devotion. These words indicate the singular attachment of Israel to its God who is in relationship with his people.[5] In the context of this attachment, God commands that the people of Israel show him their love. It may be a strange concept for some—that love can be directed—but in Judaism, it is believed to be possible, for what is emphasized is the corresponding action. Loving God is a devotion that is decreed because it can be shown in behavior, namely, by observing the commandments. With these words—known as the *shema*—Jews begin and end the day, announcing the value and coherence of the universe and the place of God within it. And if imminent death can be perceived, the words of the *shema* constitute the last declaration Jews speak before their departure from this earth.

In biblical times, the dominant competing paradigm that vied with monotheism was polytheism—a multiplicity of gods. Some were responsible for good and others for evil. Today, in contrast, agnosticism and atheism are the chief competitors to belief in one God. Nonetheless, the millennia can be bridged when we recognize that, in both ancient times and in our own, to believe that all reality is under the purview of a benevolent God who has a plan for all his creatures—commanding norms of behavior and ethics for humanity—can be immensely challenging. It is the faith of Judaism to hold fast to this truth, even when reality belies it. To believe that God is one is to assert that all of creation comes from his design and that all is purposeful and meaningful. What humans perceive as fractured, discordant, and meaningless is not only known to God but is also part of his divine plan. When people cry out, "Injustice!" God hears. Even if it cannot be seen empirically, all of creation is continuously guided by God's design—just as God created the world with the parallel structure that proclaimed his careful architecture. Perceived randomness cannot overshadow the Sovereign of the universe. The one God exists. He cares about the universe and humanity, and he will never abandon his creation.

In reading the narrative about God's creation and the first generations of human beings, we find that there are ten generations from Adam and Eve to Noah and ten generations from Noah to Abraham. This symmetry is significant, for it shows that both with humanity's first parents and with Noah, God offered paradigms for all people, showing them how to live according to his will. But both times, successive generations only increased their distance from God. Ten generations after Noah, God chose Abraham as the father of the Jewish people. From Abraham's descendants would come the next stage in God's plan to make the world a dwelling place for him. In this context, the first covenant God made with the Jewish people was for land, descendants, and blessing, promised to Abraham and Sarah.

In Jewish life, the biblical stories are never read in isolation from the rest of the vast interpretive tradition found in the literatures of the sages—the authors of the holy Jewish writings of approximately the first five centuries of the Common Era. These hallowed books include the Midrashim (Midrash, singular), the Mishnah, and the Gomorrah. (Together, the Mishnah and the Gomorrah are known as the Talmud.) It is helpful, therefore, to look at the story of Abraham as it has been done in Jewish life for thousands of years— through the perspectives of the sages. The faith of Judaism today is modeled on the first ancestor of the Jewish people, known affectionately as Abraham our Father (*Avraham Aveinu*), as his faith strengthens his descendants yet today. The extra-biblical traditions about the father of the Jewish people emphasize that he was an astronomer in Chaldea, that he grew up as the son of the infamous idol maker named Terah, that he came to believe in the one God on his own, and that he was persecuted for his beliefs (*Genesis Rabbah* 38:13). By examining the heavens, this patriarch alone could perceive, in contrast to the brilliant astronomers and astrologers of the day, that the entire universe was the creation of and under the care of the one God, who demands righteous behavior of all peoples.[6] Thus, in as much as God chose Israel to have a particular role in his plan for the world, Abraham also chose God. With Abraham's insight, for the first time humans could see that God created the heavens and the earth and the entirety of reality. God exists apart from creation and is not dependent on it. If all is created by the one God, then the entirety of the universe is unified, with God as the source of a universal morality for all humanity.[7]

As someone who came to monotheism on his own, Abraham faced a tremendous trial as the son of a Chaldean idol maker. Abraham's father, Terah, was challenged by his son to admit the folly of his beliefs. Recognizing the impediment they posed to people's faith and behavior, Abraham was compelled to smash his father's idols. This incurred his father's rage; yet, when interrogated by Terah, Abraham had the presence of mind to tell the remarkable story that one idol, being jealous of the other, brandished a club and crushed his rival. Abraham's father expressed disbelief at his son's account. Having encouraged his father to recognize the danger of idolatry, Abraham responded, "Should not your ears listen to what your mouth is saying?" (*Genesis Rabbah* 38:13). In other words, Terah unwittingly betrayed his true feelings: even he did not believe the idols contained any genuine power. Incorrigible nonetheless, Terah did not accept Abraham's perceptive revelation; the patriarch remained alone in his age as the only monotheist. Indeed, Terah, along with the brutal monarch of Chaldea—King Nimrod— began to persecute his son.

Such traditional narratives about Abraham, found in the Midrashim and in other early Jewish collections of the oral torah, show not only that God chose Abraham but also that Abraham used his own intellect to come to true knowledge of God. Such understanding, in fact, resides deep in the heart of humanity because, as the sages see it, even Abraham's idol-making father realized that the statues had no strength or power of their own. At the same time, the implications of Abraham's theology could be challenging or even frightening to others, as shown in the cruel response of King Nimrod, who hurled Abraham into a fiery furnace for his beliefs. This act, however, was met with God's rescue of the patriarch—the one who would bring knowledge of the true God to the world (*Genesis Rabbah* 38:13).

Although Abraham provides a model of belief and its significance for behavior, it is also true that faith must be one's own personal road or quest. It takes a lifetime of searching, of doing the *mitzvot* (the commandments), and of doubting—but struggling to come back to the truth—even as one confronts pain, loneliness, and tragedy. Faith is not an abstract quality; rather, it allows for a relationship with the Almighty in which one recognizes that every deed one performs matters to God and that God exercises personal providence with each individual. When people live this way, every daily act is enhanced with spirituality or elevation. That is, every ordinary deed can be infused with meaning as each person recognizes that he or she lives to carry out God's plan to make the world a dwelling place for him.

Redeemer

Throughout the first generations of the ancestors of Israel—from Abraham and Sarah to the children of Jacob—an unlikely detour took place: the people who were promised the land of Canaan, descendants, and blessing ended up as slaves in Egypt. This experience, remarkably, disclosed another aspect of the God of Israel: a God who hears the cry of the oppressed. The God who brought Israel out of Egypt is the God who redeems. When we come to the familiar story of the exodus, it is important to highlight the aspects of the account that are quintessential for Jewish interpretation of this paradigmatic event, for the narrative captures what is central for Jewish identity. Slaves, crushed in spirit, are saved by God with a particular purpose in mind: to live according to the principles of the torah. The story of the exodus reveals a God who cares and listens, even after his long silence. As God says to Moses,

> Say therefore to the Israelites, "I am the LORD, and I will free you from the burdens of the Egyptians and deliver you from slavery to them. I will redeem you with an outstretched arm and with mighty acts of judgment. I will take you as my people, and I will be your God. You shall know that I am the LORD your God, who has freed you from the burdens of the Egyptians. I will bring you into the land that I swore to give to Abraham, Isaac, and Jacob; I will give it to you for a possession. I am the LORD." Moses told this to the Israelites; but they would not listen to Moses, because of their broken spirit and their cruel slavery. (Exod 6:6-9)

With this quotation, we see the essence of the redemption from Egypt: God frees the Jewish people from bondage with a specific intent—in order to enter into a distinct relationship with them. In addition, the fulfillment of this attachment will occur in a concrete arena, namely, in the covenantal land (the land of Canaan/Israel)—promised to the ancestors. The difficulty in accepting this message is revealed by the reference to the people's brokenness, for they are too crushed to listen. Moses, nonetheless, proceeds to approach Pharaoh. Scripture says, "The LORD said to Moses, 'See, I have made you like God to Pharaoh and your brother Aaron shall be your prophet'" (Exod 7:1). Ancient Jewish commentators were struck by the reference in this verse to the god-like nature of Moses. How could this be? Here we find a window to see the importance of torah in Jewish belief. As the giver of the torah—the incomparable, central revelation to humanity—Moses was, by definition, on a higher level than any other prophet or sage.

Indeed, in ascending Mt. Sinai to receive the torah, he entered the realm of angels. Nonetheless, the exalted language was meant to show that the humble, stateless Moses was actually superior to the powerful Pharaoh—not that his own nature was divine.[8] With this, Israel learns that its mission is to serve God and not to seek the kind of power associated with Pharaoh's Egypt.

The biblical account emphasizes that Pharaoh's intransigence prevented the Hebrews from departing. Curiously, the text says not only that the Egyptian monarch "hardened his heart" but also that God, too, hardened Pharaoh's heart.[9] In Jewish thought, this was not a capricious act. One traditional explanation says that Pharaoh did not believe that his brutal actions mattered to God or that God was the final judge. Thus, the hardening of Pharaoh's heart occurred so that God could bring the plagues as a full punishment on the Egyptians for all the years of enslavement of the Jewish people. It is no surprise that the plagues included a scourge of darkness—a metaphor for the entirety of the period of slavery. Indeed, this darkness provides a spiritual link to the importance of the Passover story that continues today. In celebrating the Passover, Jews emphasize that in every generation there is darkness—defined as anything that strains the relationship that is possible with God. The distress may be because of political dangers, but even in countries that are at peace, spiritual impediments to faith exist. The celebration of Passover recognizes that in every generation, God frees each person from spiritual dismay, if only one is open to God's teachings, compassion, and forgiveness.

Thus, we find here, in essence, the story of what it means to be redeemed and a key component of Jewish self-understanding today. God undeniably responds to evil and oppression—for by nature those chains are meant to be broken. Victims and slaves can be freed. The world cries out for transformation, and truly, every commandment, even the smallest, becomes part of a larger plan for good—a plan to heal the world. This is so because of the extraordinary design of God. The story of the exodus fearlessly announces that Jews are not slaves. They are not powerless. Armed with the torah, they learn that they can strive to mend the tears in the fabric of what is good. The pharaohs of the world or the fearsome troubles of life that dominate individuals are not the masters. Only God is sovereign.

With the final plague—inflicted on the Egyptians as divine judgment—and the sparing of the Israelite firstborn comes the institution of the Passover observance. It is marked by the sacrifice of the lamb and the ritual meal, both of which are infused with religious teachings for all assembled and, in particular, for the next generation. Immediately after the institution of the commandments and traditions associated with the feast, the community sees that their God is the one who splits the Red Sea on behalf of a powerless, crushed people. Thus, the redemption from Egypt becomes a paradigm for the future salvation that will occur at the end of days. Yet, even before the event of the exodus occurs, the Israelites are told to celebrate their liberation. The chronology does not wait—the importance of teaching the narrative is stressed even while Jews are still slaves. The defining elements of this act— the God who brings light into darkness and hopelessness—is carved into the memory of the older generation, and they must now pass it on to their children. The crucial significance of Passover is noted for all future descendants:

> You shall observe this rite as a perpetual ordinance for you and your children. When you come to the land that the LORD will give you, as he has promised, you shall keep this observance. And when your children ask you, "What do you mean by this observance?" you shall say, "It is the passover sacrifice to the LORD, for he passed over the houses of the Israelites in Egypt, when he struck down the Egyptians but spared our houses." (Exod 12:24-27)

Moved by their suffering, God liberated Israel from slavery, but he also saved them for this essential reason: to become servants to him. (In Hebrew, the word for slave and servant [eved] is the same; thus one could say that Jews were saved from being slaves to Pharaoh only to become slaves to God.) Freedom is not freedom for merely its own sake, but is granted for a particular purpose: to serve God according to his unique plan that was revealed on Mt. Sinai. At this auspicious place, God promised, "I will dwell among the Israelites, and I will be their God. And they shall know that I am the LORD their God, who brought them out of the land of Egypt that I might dwell among them; I am the LORD their God" (Exod 29:45-46). Israel agrees to accept God's covenant at Sinai—the revelation of his instruction—and God reveals himself in a new way by his word (in the commandments), by dwelling among them in the sanctuary, and by guiding the people to the holy land where they will live out the specifics of his plan. They will live by his torah as servants of God—a holy, designated people.

The redemption from Egypt marked the end of an extended period of God's absence. Israel learned that God is loyal to his covenant with Abraham, even after a long silence and apparent abandonment. Moreover, the exodus is not something that only occurred once in time. Every year, when celebrating Passover, Jews read the Haggadah—the story of the exodus—based on the traditions from both the written torah and the oral torah. As the Haggadah says, "For it was not one enemy alone who rose up against us to destroy us; in every generation there are those who rise up against us and seek to destroy us. But the Holy One, blessed be He, saves us from their hands."[10] Every rescue from oppression throughout history is seen as God's intervention. But there is more. In popular etymology, the Hebrew word for Egypt, *"Mitzraim,"* means "to constrict." Thus, the sojourn in Egypt is not only about suffering during a unique time and in a particular place. Even today, all individuals must consider themselves as being person- ally redeemed. Egypt transcends time and space, for it represents anything that constricts a person's relationship with God. With God's help and grace, individuals are spared a life of slavery, however it may be defined. Physical and spiritual, imposed from outside or coming from within—anything that keeps one from an intimate relationship with God is one's Egypt. To be free from such fetters, Jews turn to their Redeemer and await the final redemp- tion at the end of days.

Revealer

As the One who gave the torah at Mt. Sinai after the exodus from Egypt, God became known to the Jewish people as Revealer—the One who gave them a blueprint for living. Judaism sees torah as a great gift that God gave to Israel, for these sacred teachings show how to connect with the Almighty in every aspect of life, from the seemingly most mundane deeds to acts of the highest spiritual significance. Indeed, the entire world is infused with the divine relationship, and the torah demonstrates the concrete expression of God's caring association with the Jewish people.

According to Jewish tradition, the torah was given in two forms: the oral torah and the written torah. The written torah refers to all the instruction Moses received at Mt. Sinai, and, by extension, to the entire (Jewish) Bible. God also gave the key for understanding the written torah: the oral torah. The oral torah consists of all the explanations and expansions of the written torah. In traditional Jewish belief, it is held that God also revealed the oral torah to Moses at Mt. Sinai. It was passed down from Moses to Joshua, to the elders, to the prophets, to the Men of the Great Assembly (the sages and religious leaders between the post-biblical and rabbinic periods). Each gener- ation faithfully transmitted it orally to the next until the Jewish revolt against Roman rule and its catastrophic reprisals prompted an urgency to write it down (Mishnah *Avot* 1:1). Thus, from approximately 200 to 600 of the

Common Era (CE [AD]), the great collections of the oral torah, the Midrashim, the Mishnah, and the Talmud became written texts. These collections are essential for understanding the written torah, as there is no "faith of the Hebrew Scriptures/Old Testament"; rather, in Judaism, the Bible is read only within the context of its hallowed, extensive commentaries.

In addition to believing that the oral teachings were handed down from Moses to subsequent generations, Judaism understands not only that specific elucidations were passed on but also that principles of interpretation originated at Sinai. Thus, the oral torah grew over the centuries, expanding to address new situations and to answer the unique questions of later generations. Living a modern life with an eye to torah values continues today, based on the experience of generations who would never go forward without looking back to God's teachings and to Jewish traditions.

The writings that comprise the oral traditions are vast. The Talmud alone fills more than twenty oversized volumes, consisting of more than sixty tractates and at least five hundred chapters. Judaism considers that a lifetime of study is insufficient to grasp it. Throughout the centuries of the compilation of the oral torah, however, certain teachers are revered as having had the ability to succinctly codify key beliefs. One such teacher, Moses ben Maimon (1135–1204), also known as Maimonides or as the Rambam, compiled core beliefs that he gleaned from the holy books. Over the centuries, the list of this prolific twelfth-century philosopher has become known as "The Thirteen Principles of Faith." Recited in the Jewish liturgy, they provide one summary of the essence of Jewish faith as it has been expressed during the past eight hundred years.[11]

1. *God is Creator*. Although he cannot be fully understood by a limited humanity, it is an article of faith in Judaism that he exists; God corresponds to a fundamental reality and is not a projection of the human mind. No formal proofs of God's existence are offered in the Bible or in the writings of the sages; this faith is presupposed. It is also true, however, that Jewish interpretation underscores that God's torah was revealed to the entirety of the Jewish people—all of whom witnessed the event: "When all the people witnessed the thunder and lightning, the sound of the trumpet, and the mountain smoking, they were afraid and trembled and stood at a distance . . . . The LORD said to Moses: Thus you shall say to the Israelites: 'You have seen for yourselves that I spoke with you from heaven . . .'" (Exod 20:18-22).

2. *God is one*. God is the Creator and sustainer of the universe and the source of all morality and ethics. Any description of God's attributes is only

to assist the finite human mind. In Jewish teaching, God is indivisible, a complete unity who cannot be apportioned into elements or parts. There is neither any theology of Trinity nor any polytheistic manifestations of God. As the following verse illustrates, there is no reality that competes with God; there is no power alongside or above him. As Moses says to his people, "So acknowledge today and take to heart that the LORD is God in heaven above and on the earth beneath; there is no other" (Deut 4:39).

In addition, in Jewish teaching there is no separate deity or divine source who creates evil; Judaism rejects dualism. Although rabbinic material does refer to Satan who tempts human beings, he is not seen as being an independent source of evil or creator of wickedness in the world. In all its difficulty, God's words to Isaiah stand: "I form light and create darkness, I make weal and create woe; I the LORD do all these things" (Isa 45:7). At the same time, Judaism teaches that each person is endowed with "a good inclination" and "an evil inclination." As creatures of free will, humans have the capacity for love and loyalty and yet also for unspeakable perversion of what is good, using what is intended for good to participate in radical evil.

3. *God is incorporeal.* Unlike humanity, God has no physical form. Although the torah and the Talmud use anthropomorphic depictions of God, they are understood to be metaphorical statements. Jews do not represent God with any physical form in art or in liturgical practices. In addition, Judaism notes that God is neither male nor female. While it is true that the gender of the names of God (YHWH, LORD, God Almighty) is masculine, this is a feature of the Hebrew language, which (like English) has no neuter pronoun. (Note that although some non-Jews vocalize the personal name of God as "Y-a-h-w-e-h," Jews normally will not pronounce this name out of respect for its sanctity.) At the same time, feminine imagery of God is present alongside masculine metaphors in the totality of the tradition. For example, Judaism speaks of the loving presence of God as "the *Shekinah*"— God's indwelling, which is a feminine noun.[12]

4. *God is eternal.* God was not created in time and has neither beginning nor end. Indeed, God transcends time and space. Thus, humans can always call on God. God reveals his name to Moses as "I AM WHO I AM" (Exod 3:14). This enigmatic phrase both reveals and conceals; the phrase can also be translated "I will be who I will be" or "I will cause to be what I will cause to be." While humans can approach God, he cannot be defined or controlled by humanity's desires. Linked with this concept are the essential ideas that God is omnipotent and omnipresent. God's omnipotence refers to the belief

that nothing is beyond God's scope or power. God is omnipresent in that there is no aspect of the universe that is devoid of his presence. Although humans are mystified and aggrieved by the inscrutability of God, it is part of Jewish belief that everything in the universe is subject to God's design.

5. *All prayer is to be offered to God alone.* Noting that God goes beyond humans' ability to speak about him, Judaism includes the prohibition against idolatry in its Ten Commandments. Idolatry is the attempt to capture God in one definable image, but it is impossible to bridge the gulf that exists between God and humanity. In addition, Judaism does not believe that prayer should be directed to any intermediaries. The story of the biblical Job is instructive. When the innocent Job demands an audience with the Almighty, remarkably, God appears. Yet God never explains to Job why he suffers. Nevertheless, he graciously reveals to Job that his beleaguered soul can never understand who God is because fathoming the reasons for suffering and struggle lie outside the realm of mere human capacities. By realizing this truth, Job is able to change his attitude from consternation and grief to humble acceptance:

> Therefore I have uttered what I did not understand,
>   things too wonderful for me, which I did not know. . . .
> I had heard of you by the hearing of the ear,
> but now my eye sees you;
>   therefore I despise myself,
>   and repent in dust and ashes. (Job 42:3-6)

In the modern world, whenever human beings idolize one value or goal over all others, making it the *sine qua non* of existence, it is akin to idolatry. What might such idols be? As Neil Gillman explains, "It need not be a material object; it can be something much more abstract or elusive: a nation, history itself (as in Marxism), financial reward, or another human being. . . . [Idolatry is reducing] God to something that cannot bear the burden of ultimacy, of transcendence. That's idolatry."[13]

6. *The directives of the prophets are true.* Judaism believes that God's will was made known to the world through the sayings of the prophets from the biblical age. The modern Jewish philosopher Abraham Joshua Heschel explains the significance of the prophets' pronouncements in ancient Israel:

> The prophets proclaimed that justice is omnipotent, that right and wrong are dimensions of world history, not merely modes of conduct. The

existence of the world is contingent upon right and wrong, and its secret is God's involvement in history. History is a turmoil. Survival and perdition are equally possible. But justice will decide; righteousness will redeem . . . justice is like a mighty stream, and to defy it is to block God's almighty surge.[14]

The age of prophecy ended during the time of Malachi (c. 500–450 BCE); yet the prophetic call to righteousness is eternal. It is now the human task to keep open the possibility of communication between God and his creation. This can be accomplished through prayer, torah study, and good deeds.

7. *Moses is the greatest prophet.* The teachings of Moses—the giver of the torah—are true, and none surpass him. This belief safeguards the primacy of torah as the source of God's will for the Jewish people.

8. *The written* torah *and the oral* torah *were given to Moses.* This statement underscores the divine origins and immutability of Jewish teachings. At the same time, it is also an essential element in Jewish belief that the principles of torah interpretation are divinely inspired. By using these norms, Jews can adapt the living tradition of torah to new situations. Such wellsprings of interpretation alert the community to the intentions brought to bear when engaging in behavior. The oral torah evidences an outlook in which common, ordinary materials and actions take on a heightened awareness, infused with spirituality. Jews strive to be on the alert to find God in the most mundane activities. Everyday actions can be sanctified.

Let us consider, for example, the discussion of food containers in Jewish law. Examining the teachings of Rabbinic Judaism, we see how, in antiquity, ordinary Jews strove to make their homes a place for the indwelling of God's presence. In light of the destruction of the second temple (c. 70 CE), the people no longer had an altar for sacrifice; yet the family table became the locus of sanctification. Jacob Neusner explains that this could occur because of the peoples' way of looking at the world—the manner in which they considered every act of living and being. What marked the community was a "perpetual awareness, an always-active intentionality . . . . Utensils [used for the cooking and serving of meals] made a difference because food was prepared in and eaten from them, so at stake in the end is sustaining life in conditions of holiness, so far as these can be attained."[15] By organizing and categorizing what is found in the empirical world, the sages of the formative period of Judaism developed an extensive system of behavior and ethics that continues to be essential for the identity of the Jewish people.

9. *The torah will never be superseded.* As do the previous two statements of belief, this statement highlights the importance of revelation in time. Because Judaism holds that God revealed both the written and the oral torah, torah is never static—it is a living tradition that constantly calls out to be interpreted.

10. *God knows the thoughts and actions of human beings.* God is omniscient and directs the world through his providence. This belief holds that God is the true judge who knows the entirety of human behavior; actions have consequences in the divine scale of justice. At the same time, God draws near to human beings. Always inscrutable, he nonetheless is involved with humans in close relationship.

Thus, although God is unknowable in his essence, Judaism holds that in revelation God can indeed be discovered, all the while in mystery. God cannot be described; God cannot be spoken to directly (even Moses was veiled), but God has shown that he loves and cares for humanity and is the author of a meaningful, purposeful world. Using the metaphor of a veil, David Gerlernter clarifies, "If God and Man face each other with a veil in between, they are face to face yet not face to face. The veil allows transcendence and intimacy to coexist. It hides God's presence but not his nearness."[16]

11. *God rewards the righteous and punishes evildoers.* Judaism holds that there is a world to come in which all are judged according to their merits. At the same time, the Almighty is a God not only of justice but also of mercy. Indeed, the names of God used in the Bible, in particular "The LORD" (YHWH) and "God" (Elohim), are seen as representing his attributes of mercy and justice, respectively.

12. *God will send a messiah.* Judaism teaches that it is part of the divine plan for the perfection of the world that God's anointed, a descendant of David, will come to redeem the world. We will study the Jewish understanding of the messiah in chapter 2 below.

13. *God will resurrect the dead.* Judaism holds that the soul is eternal and will be joined again with the body in the world to come. Each individual is both physical and spiritual—with each aspect endowed with infinite significance. This idea is explored in chapter 2 as well.

Maimonides' approach, which never limits the transcendence of God, allows his essence—which is unknowable—to remain in ultimate mystery. Indeed, no approach is ever complete or comprehensive. But Judaism also holds that God is not simply the sum of what he is not. Maimonides' principles of faith appeal to rational or logical attempts to categorize essential Jewish beliefs. An alternative approach captures the more mystical ways of articulating the faith of Judaism. This tradition is known as Kabbalah, a system of deliberation on the torah that explores the way in which God relates to the world not only as its Creator but also as it Maintainer. Isaac Luria (1534–1572) emphasized that everyone could appreciate the wisdom of the Zohar, an ancient mystical text that—tradition teaches—has its origins with Shimon Bar Yochai in the first century CE. This work delineates the mystical meaning of the torah, emphasizing God's immanence and transcendence in all aspects of life.

Kabbalistic teaching emphasizes that human beings cannot possibly fathom God's essence. By an act of God's graciousness, however, he has allowed us to discern indications of his infinite power, will, and plan for the universe. These indications are known through a system of *sefirot*, spheres or manifestations of aspects of God's being that he allows people to perceive. The words that categorize these divine abodes of existence are telling. They are identified as follows: God's power or crown; wisdom (God's plan for the world); intelligence or understanding; mercy or lovingkindness; power (God's judgment and law); beauty; victory; splendor; the foundation of the world (that allows all revelation to come into existence within the totality of God's transcendent and physical worlds); and presence or kingdom (*shekinah*), "the feminine aspect of God" that enables all of God's creative processes to be perceived on earth.[17] This terminology is inspired by the following verse of Scripture: "Yours, O LORD, are the greatness, the power, the glory, the victory, and the majesty; for all that is in the heavens and on the earth is yours; yours is the kingdom, O LORD, and you are exalted as head above all" (1 Chr 29:11). Isaac Luria called to the forefront of Jewish teaching the concepts of contraction (*tzimtzum*) and repair (*tikkun*). We turn now to an outline of these inspiring teachings.[18]

In the course of creating the world, God's light and presence were so overwhelmingly vast that he had to diminish his own presence, making room for the created order. God's light was gathered into ten vessels—ten gifts that would make his presence known in the world. As Ronald Isaacs says, "By this act of withdrawal, God made room for the world by retreating from a portion of his universe. By retreating, God gave people the freedom to exist on their own and to choose between good and evil."[19] Yet the vessels were too fragile to contain his powerful presence. Upon entering the world, they shattered, sending the sparks of godliness throughout creation, encased in concealment. Thus, the world that we find is imperfect, broken, and marked by evil. The Jewish task is clear: all must work not only to choose good and avoid evil but also to participate actively in the repair of the world. Because God's desire was that the world be filled with goodness, the community must gather up the sparks of the divine presence, repairing the brokenness of the world and showing its every corner that there are holy embers that must be revealed. Every teaching studied and every commandment followed has a real effect on the condition of this fractured world, rendering it less wounded. By collecting the divine sparks, and by giving them back to God, people can participate in the renewal and healing of the world. How is this accomplished? By obedience to the commandments, by service of God (prayer), and by acts of kindness, one's soul can be elevated, allowing for a bond with God that helps to realize this restoration of the world.

Despite its complex and detailed language, the main idea of Kabbalistic teaching is this: because God's dwelling in the universe has been dispersed, the world is in sore need of healing. God's essence is likened to a vessel of sparks that has been shattered. It is the task of human beings to collect the divine fragments of light, to mend the vessels, and to bring these embers of the divine presence back to God. In this way, a hidden radiance—a concealed goodness—can become visible in the world. In effect, humanity partners with God in redeeming the world, for no place is devoid of his presence.

Judaism teaches that God's actions in the world are part of an intricate design; God does not operate via random fiat. There are laws of nature and providence in history—all signs of God's care. In the context of his love, God gave the torah to Israel, showing the details of his design for the universe and for Israel's place within his plan. Torah forms a bridge between God and humanity, for divine wisdom is revealed in its teachings.

Theodicy

Despite the logic and beauty of these teachings, Judaism does not hide from the existential question: if a compassionate and just God exists, with a profoundly detailed plan for good, why is there suffering? Questions of theodicy—literally, God's justice—have been raised in Jewish texts from biblical times to the present. By examining the Mishnah's account of one of the journeys of Rabbi Akiva (c. 50–135 CE) and the commentary of Rashi (1040–1105 CE) on the burning bush (Exod 3:1-15), we now turn to two examples of the approaches that Judaism brings to these timeless complexities. These narratives pose the question that, to be sure, can never fully be understood. Only through the eyes of faith does Judaism declare that God's goodness and providence remain intact even when circumstances belie this belief. Sometimes meaning can be found in retrospect, but at other times, the silence continues as far as humans can discern.

Traveling a long distance and stopping for the night, Rabbi Akiva found that he could not get a room at the town's inn. Giving him no other choice but to sleep by the side of the road, the evening could not have progressed any worse. A lion killed his donkey, a wild cat devoured his rooster, and the wind blew out his lamp. Rabbi Akiva comforted himself each time by saying, "Whatever God does, he does for the best." Only later, with the morning light, did Akiva discover that marauders had raided the inn, murdering all inside. By losing his animals and by having the light extinguished, Akiva remained hidden. Judaism affirms the existence of human free will but at the same time underscores that when bad things happen, humans are not always able to evaluate them from a proper standpoint since humanity's vision is limited only to the present. Sometimes it is the case that only within the context of a larger perspective can people discern the ultimate results of events, which may prove to be a force for good in the end. Rabbi Akiva's trials illustrate this. Everything that befell him was frightening when it occurred, but the next day he learned that the events actually prevented a much worse fate; only with the daylight could Rabbi Akiva see the larger picture. Only on the next day did Akiva realize that the inn had been raided; surely, if his losses had not happened, the robbers—alerted to his presence— would have attacked him as well.[20]

To be sure, on other occasions, people are never given even a glimpse of understanding any purpose of the existence of unfathomable evils. But through the eyes of faith, Judaism audaciously declares that even in inexplicable suffering, God is present. Thus, the great commentator Rashi explores the account of the revelation of God's name at the burning bush with an eye to the depths of despair of an enslaved people who could see no rhyme or reason for their tragic fate. The circumstances that characterized Jewish life when Moses approached the burning bush could not have been more forbidding. A despotic empire had brutally enslaved the people. Babies were thrown into the Nile. Laborers were beaten. When Moses drew near to God, he inquired, "Who am I that I should go to Pharaoh, and bring the Israelites out of Egypt?" (Exod 3:11). God's answer sounds decidedly cryptic: "I AM" (Exod 3:14) sends Moses. What does this mysterious sentence mean? For Rashi, it should be understood thus: "'I, Who shall Be' with them in this suffering [am the One] 'Who will be' with them when they will be subjugated by the other kingdoms" (*Commentary on Exodus* 3:14). God does not reveal his essence, but he does give us a hint of how to understand him: in his actions. The irresolvable questions of a frightened and crushed people are never fully answered. God remains unfathomable. Yet, when God enigmatically answers Moses' question, the people learn that the Almighty is neither disconnected nor disengaged from them. He is present in their suffering, standing alongside them with every anguished cry. God's mystery remains inscrutable, but the proclamation of the Jewish people is that this infinite God is intimately involved in every act that takes place in the world. There is meaning and purpose in the world, even when we cannot see it. The recitation of *Hallel* (psalms of praise) that takes place during the liturgy reminds the community to be ever mindful of this fact. The congregation recites Psalms 113–118 to mark the beginning of each month (of the Jewish calendar) and on the holidays of Passover, Shavuot, and Sukkot. These psalms recall the redemption from Egypt, the gift of the torah, the promise of the resurrection, and the coming of the messianic age. Armed with this faith, *Hallel* also allows for the congregation to voice appeals for God's care and mercy. The following excerpt captures the essence of this important communal act of praise:

> From the rising of the sun to its setting, the Name of the Lord is praised. Who is like the Lord our God who dwells on high [yet] looks down so low upon heaven and earth! . . . I was brought low and He saved me. Return, my soul, to your tranquility, for the Lord has bestowed goodness upon you . . . . Praise the Lord, all you nations . . . . Offer praise to the Lord for He is good, for His kindness is everlasting . . . . From out of distress I called to God; with abounding relief, God answered me . . . . We implore You, Lord, deliver us. We implore You, Lord, grant us success . . . . May [the Lord] protect me and grant me life. So may it be Your will, living God and eternal King, in whose hand is the soul of every living thing.[21]

With these words the community places its life, its well-being, and its hopes into the care of a loving God.

Notes

1. Unless otherwise specified, biblical quotations are taken from the *New Oxford Annotated Bible*, ed. Bruce Metzger and Roland Murphy, New Revised Standard Version (New York: Oxford University Press, 1994).

2. Talmud, *Hagigah* 12a.

3. Howard Schwartz, *The Tree of Souls: The Mythology of Judaism* (Oxford and New York: Oxford University Press, 2004) 74–75. See also *Pirke de Rabbi Eliezer* (ed. Gerald Friedlander; New York: Hermon Press, 1970) ch. 3, p. 11.

4. Abravanel, quoted in Nehama Lebowitz, *New Studies in Shemot (Exodus)*, Part 2: Mishpatim-Pekudai, trans. Aryeh Newman (Jerusalem: Haomanim Press, 1993) 472.

5. Neil Gillman, *The Way into Encountering God in Judaism* (Woodstock VT: Jewish Lights Publishing, 2000) 18.

6. For additional references see *Jubilees* 11:16-12:7; *The Apocalypse of Abraham* 1:3; *Genesis Rabbah* 38:13.

7. Schwartz, *Tree of Souls*, 328–29.

8. James Kugel, *The Bible as It Was* (Cambridge MA: Belknap Press, 1997) 311–29.

9. God hardens Pharaoh's heart, as shown in Exod 7:3; 9:12; 10:1, 20, 27; 11:10; 14:4, 8. Pharaoh hardens his own heart as seen in 8:15, 32; 9:34. The passive construction, with no identified subject, is found in 7:13, 14, 22; 8:19; 9:7, 35.

10. *Passover Haggadah*, new rev. ed., ed. Nathan Goldberg (Hoboken NJ: Ktav, 1993) 12.

11. Maimonides, *Commentary on the Mishnah* (tractate *Sanhedrin* 10:1). See also Louis Jacobs, *The Book of Jewish Belief* (Springfield NJ: Behrman House, 1984) 5.

12. Talmud, *Sanhedrin* 39a; *Berachot* 6a; *Shabbat* 12b; *Megillah* 29a.

13. Gillman, *The Way into Encountering God*, 5.

14. Abraham J. Heschel, *The Prophets*, vol. 1 (New York: Harper and Row, 1962) 214–15.

15. Jacob Neusner, *The Comparative Hermeneutics of Rabbinic Judaism*, vol. 5, Seder Tohorot from Kelim through Parah (Binghamton NY: Academic Studies in the History of Judaism, 2000) 115.

16. David Hillel Gerlernter, *Judaism: A Way of Being* (New Haven and London: Yale, 2009) 56.

17. Schwartz, *Tree of Souls*, 9–10.

18. See Ronald Isaacs, *Close Encounters: Jewish Views about God* (Northvale NJ and London: Jason Aronson, 1996) 120–25, and Howard Schwartz, "How the Ari Created a Myth and Transformed Judaism," *Tikkun*, 28 March 2011, online at http://www.tikkun.org/nextgen/how-the-ari-created-a-myth-and-transformed-judaism (accessed 14 May 2012).

19. Isaacs, *Close Encounters*, 123–24.

20. Talmud, *Berachot* 60b. See the interpretation from Chaim Pearl, *Theology in Rabbinic Stories* (Peabody MA: Hendrickson, 2003) 120–24.

21. Nissen Mangel, ed. and trans., *Siddur Tehillat Hashem* (New York: Merkos L'Inyonei Chinuch, 1982) 241–45.

Chapter 2

Messiah, Afterlife, and Resurrection

The Messiah

I have found my servant David; with my holy oil I have anointed him . . . .
I will set his hand on the sea and his right hand on the rivers.
He shall cry to me, "You are my Father,
   my God, and the Rock of my salvation!"
I will make him the firstborn, the highest of the kings of the earth.
Forever I will keep my steadfast love for him,
   and my covenant with him will stand firm.
I will establish his line forever,
   and his throne as long as the heavens endure. (Ps 89:20-29)

Psalm 89 well captures the theology of kingship found in the Bible: the monarch is the recipient of God's covenantal loyalty and faithfulness. God made a covenant with King David and his descendants: the royal line would endure forever. The king was obligated to remain faithful to the commandments—for God's shepherd was to establish righteousness and would be punished if he sinned—but God's covenantal loyalty would be everlasting. When the royal inauguration took place, a designated prophet poured oil over the king's head; thus he was known as "God's anointed." From the verb "anoint" (*mashach*) comes the noun "the anointed one," the *mashiach*, which in English is "the messiah."

What is most striking about this theology of kingship is that the concept remained meaningful for the Jewish people even after the institution of kingship ceased during Judah's exile. While it is accurate that *mashiach* does not mean "savior" or "redeemer," it is also true that the people of Israel looked forward to the day when a righteous king would come in the future, bringing freedom from foreign oppression to Israel and knowledge of God to a peaceful world. This expectation infused the Jewish people with hope even during some of their darkest times. The words of the Hebrew prophets predicted a time when there would be a future Davidic king in a glorious age of peace and no suffering:[1]

> A shoot shall come out from the stump of Jesse,
>   and a branch shall grow out of his roots.
> The spirit of the LORD shall rest on him,
>   the spirit of wisdom and understanding,
>   the spirit of counsel and might,
>   the spirit of knowledge and the fear of the LORD. . . .
>
> Righteousness shall be the belt around his waist,
>   and faithfulness the belt around his loins.
> The wolf shall live with the lamb,
>   the leopard shall lie down with the kid,
> the calf and the lion and the fatling together,
>   and a little child shall lead them. . . .
>
> They will not hurt or destroy on all my holy mountain;
> for the earth will be full of the knowledge of the LORD
>   as the waters cover the sea. (Isa 11:1-9)

In Jewish thought, the time of this future king, this anointed one—called the age of the messiah—will be marked by the return to Israel of all Jews from throughout the exile, reunited in peace under the direction of this descendant of Jesse (King David's father). The hope for the messiah who is yet to come, who will restore Zion, and who will transform the world to be a dwelling place for God (but is not divine himself) is uttered daily in Jewish prayer. Throughout history, this hope has not only expressed a yearning for an end to suffering within the Jewish community but also conveyed an aspect of Judaism's universal outlook. Judaism's messianic expectation holds that all nations will learn about God, love him, and obey the commandments. With this understanding, the world will be transformed, becoming the peaceful creation that God designed from the beginning of time. In effect, the Jewish hope for the messiah holds that once again the world will be like Eden, marked by abundance and harmony: there will be no sorrow, suffering, or war. The entire world will so know and love God—automatically, without proselytizing—that all people will strive for peace and justice. The messiah will save all people from oppression, persecution, suffering, and anything that keeps humanity from God.

The oral torah continues the development of the biblical ideal of this paradigmatic future. The king who is to come—a true descendant of David—will be a leader of the Jewish people, designated by God for this special purpose. His mission will be to bring about the final redemption, marked by the ingathering of all Jews of the diaspora (the lands outside Israel) into the land of Israel and characterized by a time of peace and prosperity for the entire world. To this aim, the messiah will have a special mission to the poor. The Talmud records the following exchange between Rabbi Joshua ben Levi and Elijah, the prophet who will return as the harbinger of the messianic age:

> R. Joshua: "When will the Messiah come?"
> Elijah: "Go and ask him."
> R. Joshua: "Where is he sitting?"
> Elijah: "At the gates of Rome."
> R. Joshua: "What will identify him?"
> Elijah: "He is sitting among the poor lepers; while all of them untie all [their bandages] at once, and rebandage them together, he unties and rebandages each separately, [before treating the next], saying 'I might be needed, so I must not be delayed.'" (Talmud, *Sanhedrin* 98a)

This text underscores that the messiah is inextricably concerned with the suffering of this world. Even though he has not yet come in person, he is already present in the sense of being among those who work for the elimination of suffering in every age, even now. As Rabbi Chaim Pearl says of this exchange, the messiah "is present among mankind helping to relieve the pain and the afflictions of a bruised humankind."[2] Nonetheless, Jewish teaching warns the community to be cautious about believing that the final redemption has already come. For example, Maimonides notes the following way in which the community will know whether the messiah has arrived:

> If a king from the House of David studies Torah, busies himself with the commandments like David did, observes the laws of the written and the oral law, convinces Israel to walk in the way of the Torah and to repair its breaches, and fights the battles of the Lord, it may be assumed that he is the Messiah. If he succeeds at these things, rebuilds the Temple on its site, and gathers the dispersed of Israel, he is beyond all doubt the Messiah . . . . But if he does not succeed fully, or is slain, it is obvious that he is not the Messiah promised in the Torah. (*Laws of Kings* 11:3-4)

Some passages in the oral torah state that the age of the messiah will also be marked by the extraordinary and the miraculous. The third temple will be rebuilt and the sacrificial system reinstituted, cataclysmic events will be seen in nature, and the resurrection of the dead will occur. Interpretations range from the literal to the figurative. Maimonides does not stress the supernatural aspects that may accompany the messiah but rather the perfection of the world that will occur through his modeling of torah observance. He remarks,

> The world will not change its accustomed order, but Israel will dwell secure, and humanity will find that true faith which will prevent them from making war and carrying destruction. Israel will not become exalted over humanity or wield power, but will be undisturbed to follow Torah, study it, perfect its Mitzvot. No longer will there be war in the world; all humanity will enjoy peace and prosperity; and all will search for that wisdom which God alone can give. (*Mishneh Torah* 11.12)

Maimonides' twelfth principle of faith underscores the importance of belief in the messiah that continues today: "I believe with full faith in the coming of the Messiah. No matter how long it takes, I will await his coming."[3] Throughout the history of the dispersion of Israel, belief in a messianic age or in an individual messiah has been a central tenet of Judaism, inspiring Jews even in the worst times of oppression, catastrophe, and tyranny. This hope for an end to suffering and to be in the land of Zion reveals an essential element of Jewish teaching: that the truths of torah will indeed become clearly manifest; a time will come when God will no longer be concealed. People can have hope for a deeper relationship with God, who will right the wrongs of the world in such a way that the entirety of creation reflects his presence. Even when their communities were decimated, expelled, imprisoned, or enslaved, Jews continued to believe that God was the Master of history and would bring about the redemption of the world. As Rabbi Leo Trepp remarks, with this inspiration of the messianic hope, Jews have looked forward to "wholeheartedly responding to the divine call in Mitzvah [doing the commandments and good deeds]. . . . [The messianic hope] was transposed into the future as both goal and challenge."[4] His words are particularly moving since Rabbi Trepp himself was a holocaust survivor.

Instead of a personal messiah, liberal branches of Judaism are more likely to anticipate a messianic kingdom or messianic age. The Reform Jewish movement, which began in nineteenth-century Germany, strives to combine traditional Jewish thought with modernity, believing that the laws of the oral torah—although significant—are not binding. In its 1885 Pittsburg Platform, which articulated key principles, the Reform Movement modulated the traditional teaching of the coming of an heir of King David. Reform Jews more commonly speak of the coming of the *redemption* as opposed to a *redeemer*. The words of the Jewish philosopher, Hermann Cohen, are telling:

> . . . the symbol of the Messiah, is . . . the goal, it is the meaning of history. It is humanity itself which has to bring about the age of the Messiah . . . the ideal of human life, the ideal of individuals and nations, the future of the Messiah . . . the realization of morality on earth, its tasks and its eternal goal, this, and nothing else is the meaning of the messiah for us.[5]

Reflecting on the function of the messianic hope, Steven Katz explains that in the age of the messiah,

> . . . all of this suffering will find some redemption. Human history, for all of the very real counterevidences, will finally be set right and there will be a just government, a caring government, a government for the people [and] at some future time Creation will be taken up in God's hands and remade with the kind of perfection that all of us would wish it to have.[6]

This vision of the world continues to inspire Jews in their daily lives. One of the emphases of the Jewish teachings on the messiah is that every individual has the capacity to encourage his coming. By obeying the commandments, by making the world a dwelling place for God, humankind can help to usher in an age of redemption by their own actions. As Zalman Schacter-Shalomi writes, belief in the messiah is "the Jewish way of daring to hope that the future will be better than anything we have experienced so far. . . . We all carry the sparks of Mashiach. We all, in our unassuming ways, can work to improve the world."[7] By imagining a better world, people can help to make real what otherwise might be dismissed as a utopian ideal. These quotations underscore the Jewish idea of a purposeful world. This real, material, physical world has intrinsic value and can become a dwelling place for God that the entirety of the world will see.

Although Judaism teaches that every person can work for the repair and perfection of the world, it also underscores that only the Sovereign of the universe can bring the time of the messiah into reality. Humans cannot perfect the world on their own; nor can humans force the hand of God, because humankind is, sadly, marked by hatred, violence, and cruelty. Still, God's creation is intended for good. Steven Schwarzschild emphasizes that although a huge gulf separates humanity from its transformation for good, humans can continuously strive for perfection—with God's help. He explains,

> In the Garden of Eden, in [man's] original, primordial existence he actually possessed the conditions intended for him, but from the outset he abused the very divine-like qualities given to him for immoral and impious purposes. Ever since, God has offered man the means with which to reconstitute himself and his environment so that he will conform to the image which he was meant to present and which he himself senses to be his ideal condition. The means offered to him to achieve this goal is God's law, but the defects in his character which caused his original deviation continue to disable him for fulfilling the law. At best man is limited and fallible, and at worst sinful. If man's destination, on the other hand, is perfection, this perfection cannot, therefore, in its nature, be brought about by man. It must be accomplished by God. . . . human salvation is a miracle, something which by the laws of nature and logic is impossible.[8]

No single human being, no particular government, no particular political or social philosophy that exists today can perfect humankind. The belief in the messiah as a singular human being, who comes because God wills it, reminds humanity of this fact. What must people do in the meantime, while awaiting the final redemption? Schwarzschild continues,

> Redemption always remains in the hands of God and is undeserved by imperfect men. But men do play a significant part in the drama of salvation, and they can affect its denouement by their lives…the characteristics of the Messianic kingdom are regarded as commandments for daily living; they, as it were, anticipate the world-to-come in this world.[9]

In short, every act of torah learning, every act of kindness, every act of giving charity, every pursuit of justice, helps to change the world. Jews continue to express the hope that humanity can tip the balance, so to speak, of preparing the world to receive the messiah, no matter the differences among Orthodox and Reform in understanding the individual messiah or the character of the messianic age.

The Afterlife

Because all people face suffering and death, it is natural to ask whether the quest for meaning will end unanswered, or whether life will continue with God in some yet unknowable way. Judaism addresses this issue in its texts that deal with resurrection, immortality, and the afterlife. In Jewish teaching, resurrection is understood as the restoration of the life of the body after death; immortality refers to the eternal existence of the soul; and the afterlife speaks of personal existence in the world to come. These topics may be referred to separately or may be linked with each other in Jewish thought. Traditional Jewish teaching holds that God will judge body and soul inseparably as deserving either punishment or reward at the end of days, the time ushered in by the messiah. The development of the idea was marked by disagreement in antiquity, but the teaching of Orthodox Judaism today is that when the body dies, the soul continues on in the afterlife, awaiting the resurrection of the body.

A number of key verses (from both the written and oral torah) are understood, in traditional interpretation, to exemplify the teaching on resurrection. First, we consider this quotation from the book of Daniel:

> At that time Michael, the great prince, the protector of your people, shall arise. There shall be a time of anguish, such as has never occurred since nations first came into existence. But at that time your people shall be delivered, everyone who is found written in the book. Many of those who sleep in the dust of the earth shall awake, some to everlasting life, and some to shame and everlasting contempt. Those who are wise shall shine like the brightness of the sky, and those who lead many to righteousness, like the stars forever and ever. (Dan 12:1-3)

The historical context of the book of Daniel was the terrible times of oppression under Antiochus IV, the Syrian-Greek ruler who outlawed Jewish practice (c. 165 BCE). Daniel's vision looks to the time to come, when the terrible injustices of the world will be made right—when the "holy ones of the Most High shall receive the kingdom" (Dan 7:18). Suffering will mark this epoch at first, but it will also be a time of God's judgment. The language is poetic, but we can see that a positive, although unspecified, transcendent reality awaits the righteous. Although Daniel 12 speaks of the everlasting punishment of the wicked, Judaism came more commonly to teach that evil souls are completely cut off from the presence of God rather than being infinitely tormented. (It is important to remember that all references to the afterlife are poetic and symbolic; there is no "official teaching.") Thus, *Gehinnom* (hell) is understood to be a place of purification for righteous souls who yet need to atone for their shortcomings before they appear before God in the afterlife. Here the soul experiences regret for the harm caused to others and for lost occasions to perform righteous deeds. The image of *Gehinnom* has roots in biblical times; it originally referred to the horrific place of child sacrifice to the ancient Ammonite god Molech, condemned in the torah and by Israel's prophets (Lev 18:21; Jer 7:31; 19:4-5; 32:35). Jewish teaching uses the metaphor of a year as the time limit during which the soul atones for its sins in *Gehinnom* before enjoying God's presence.

Next, we consider verses from the prophets Isaiah and Ezekiel. Isaiah proclaims, "Your dead shall live, their corpses shall arise. O dwellers in the dust, awake and sing for joy!" (Isa 26:19). On one level, the context of these words was the time of the great devastation that the empire of Assyria (722 BCE) inflicted on Israel. Traditional Jewish teaching, however, is that Isaiah is also speaking about the reality of death that strikes all people—one that will be followed by the world to come. Isaiah's vision is that God does not abandon his people, even when the current reality of suffering and death appears to belie this belief. Similar to the era of devastation wrought by Assyria, the times of the Babylonian exile (late sixth century BCE) were at least as terrible—if not more so.

In this context, the prophet Ezekiel had a vision of dry bones being resurrected. God gave these words to the exilic prophet, explaining the vision:

> Then he said to me, "Mortal, these bones are the whole house of Israel. They say, 'Our bones are dried up, and our hope is lost; we are cut off completely.' Therefore prophesy, and say to them, Thus says the Lord GOD: I am going to open your graves, and bring you up from your graves, O my people; and I will bring you back to the land of Israel. And you shall know that I am the LORD, when I open your graves, and bring you up from your graves, O my people. I will put my spirit within you, and you shall live, and I will place you on your own soil; then you shall know that I, the LORD, have spoken and will act, says the LORD." (Ezek 37:11-14)

In Jewish thought, this text not only refers to the continuing existence of the Jewish people after the Babylonian exile but also attests to the existence of resurrection for all, across time. Although this biblical passage may strike the skeptic as fanciful, resurrection is an article of faith that is based on the understanding of an omnipotent God. Surely, if God can create and sustain the world, he can breathe life into the dead once again. Maurice Lamm notes the connection between the life-sustaining acts of God in this world and the Jewish hope for resurrection, as reflected in the Eighteen Benedictions, said in daily prayer:

> You are mighty forever, my Lord; You resurrect the dead; You are powerful to save. [In winter the congregation says:] He causes the wind to blow and the rain to fall. [In summer:] He causes the dew to descend. He sustains the living with lovingkindness, resurrects the dead with great mercy, supports the falling, heals the sick, releases the bound, and fulfills His trust to those who sleep in the dust. . . . who can be compared to You, King, who brings death and restores life, and causes deliverance to spring forth![10]

Note that in this prayer an analogy is made between hope for the resurrection of the dead and evidence of a sustaining God who gives rain and dew to maintain life.[11] In addition, God's great acts of mercy to those broken by illness, imprisonment, or poverty also attest to the salvation that God grants—both in this world and in the hereafter.

With these biblical texts that set the context of rabbinic thinking, we find the following teaching in the Mishnah (2nd century CE), insisting on the reality of the World to Come (the *Olam Ha Ba*) and on the belief of the resurrection.

> All Israel have a portion in the World to Come, for it is written, "Thy people are all righteous; they shall inherit the land for ever, the branch of my planting, the work of my hands, that I may be glorified." [Isa 60:21] But the following have no portion therein: he who maintains that resurrection is not a biblical doctrine, the Torah was not divinely revealed, and an *epikoros* [skeptic]. (Mishnah, *Sanhedrin* 10:1)

This text proclaims that there is a World to Come for all of Israel—meaning all those who obey God's laws and believe in the God who judges all. Although this text addresses Jews alone, it is important to remember that at the time it was written, their Roman rulers were oppressors who had waged war against them, inflicting torture, death, and slavery. Other rabbinic texts teach that the World to Come is open to all righteous persons, and Maimonides held as well that "the pious of the nations of the world have a place in the world to come."[12]

We next turn to this Talmudic passage, which underscores the teaching on resurrection found in the Mishnah:

How do we know that the resurrection of the dead can be derived from the Torah? From the verse, "I also established My covenant with them [i.e., Abraham, Isaac, and Jacob], *to* give *them* the land of Canaan" (Exod. 6, 4). "To you" is not written but "*to them.*" Hence, resurrection of the dead can be derived from the Torah. (Talmud, *Sanhedrin* 90b)[13]

Here, Rabbi Simai looks at a biblical text, namely Exodus 6:4, in which God tells Moses that he gave a covenant to the patriarchs. Rabbi Simai recognizes that God's promise was not yet realized during their own lifetimes. Therefore, the sage reasons, God will fulfill his covenantal promise to Israel's founding fathers in the future—at some point after their resurrection. In another rabbinic text, we find that the conception of the resurrection of the dead is associated with the final redemption, of which the exodus is a fore-taste. In commenting on the torah's presentation of the exodus, Rabbi Yehuda Ha-Nasi argues that the opening verse of the Song of the Sea (the song of thanksgiving recited after the crossing of the Red Sea), which reads, "Moses *sang* [to the LORD]" should rather be read as follows, "Then Moses *will sing* [to the LORD]" (Exod 15:1; *Mekhilta Shirata* 1). In other words, Moses' words of praise to God cannot be given until the lawgiver himself is resurrected from the dead and experiences the final redemption. Thus, the significance of this text lies in the future, attesting to God's plan.

What happens between the time of death and resurrection? In the following Talmudic reference, we find an emphasis on the spiritual and unfathomable character of the afterlife and on the continuation of one's eternal soul: "In the future world there is no eating, drinking, propagation, business, jealously, hatred or competition, but the righteous sit, with their crown on their heads, enjoying the brilliance of the Shechinah [divine presence]" (Talmud, *Berakhot* 17a).

In Jewish thought, the soul continues throughout the period between death and resurrection. Life does not end at death. The incorporeal soul, the very essence of life, is eternal—existing as pure spirit before God places it in a body, and reconnecting with its Source, with God, after death. In the daily prayers, Jews say, "My God, the soul which You have given me is pure. You have created it, You have formed it, You have breathed it into me, and You preserve it within me. You will eventually take it from me, and restore it within me in the Time to Come."[14]

Judaism teaches that on earth good deeds draw people nearer to God, forming a relationship that continues infinitely in the hereafter. Thus, the Mishnah speaks of this world as being an antechamber of the world to come:

"This world is like a vestibule before the world to come; prepare thyself in the vestibule that thou mayest enter into the hall" (Mishnah, *Avot* 4:21).

On the one hand, human action on earth is crucially important for its own sake. By following the commandments, one can participate in God's essence and goodness. On the other hand, this world is also a preparatory realm for ultimate reunification with God. The life that humanity encounters on earth is based on corporeal existence. But in contrast to the provisional and impermanent experiences of life in this world, an eternal life awaits the immortal part—the soul—of each individual. The soul's reward is the ability to merge with the divine when it is freed from its material constraints. This is the reward to the righteous after death. Nonetheless, Judaism does not emphasize that people should do the right thing primarily or only because deeds are rewarded in the hereafter. As the Mishnah states, "Be not like servants who serve their master for the sake of receiving a reward; instead, be like servants who serve their master not for the sake of receiving a reward, and let the awe of Heaven [God] be upon you" (*Avot* 1:3). One can experience a glimpse of eternity in the present by doing the right thing for its own sake. While it is true that Judaism believes that all good deeds are rewarded in the world to come, it is also true that *this very world* is good and that humanity can help make *this world* a dwelling place for God.

There is disagreement among Jewish thinkers regarding the permanence of the resurrected state. Maimonides held that with the resurrection, all the righteous will enjoy the times of the messiah, the final redemption. This period, nonetheless, will not be marked by the supernatural. Rather, the resurrected souls will enjoy the time of peace that the messiah brings, but their bodies will die again; only their souls are to experience eternal life. The medieval torah scholar, Nachmanides (1195–1270), however, taught that the resurrection referred to a permanent state, although ultimately unfathomable, since we are referring to an otherworldly reality. For Jewish thinkers who follow Nachmanides' lead, the time of the resurrection is the ultimate link between the spiritual and material. This theology completely underscores the crucial importance of finding God in the physical, material world because this reality is neither a passing phenomenon nor a temporary trial to endure. It is of ultimate worth and value as a home of the divine. The world reflects God's presence and purpose; the resurrection of the body and its reunification with the soul is a logical consequence, so to speak, of the value of this world as a place for God.[15]

The sages taught that the beliefs in the continuation of the soul after death and in the resurrection of the body are ultimately a mystery. While it is an article of faith that the existence people have on earth is not all there is, it is also true that anything but a veiled understanding of life with God after death is impossible. The reward promised to the righteous addresses the problem of suffering in this world, but Judaism holds that it is not a sufficient or complete answer, for it, too, cannot be grasped by the human mind. Ultimately, the reasons for evil and suffering are known to God alone. The human task is to respond to evil—to find meaning as we work for the betterment of the world, trusting that it is redeemable. Surely an individual can question, crying out to God from the depths of one's soul, giving voice to one's anguish. Ultimately, because God's ways are inscrutable, gaps in human understanding will remain.[16] The faith of the Jewish people evidences that both the spiritual and material are holy. Both soul and body are the creations of God. As Maurice Lamm states, "Resurrection affirms that the body is of value because it came from God, and it will be revived by God. Resurrection affirms that man's empirical existence is valuable in God's eyes."[17]

In common Jewish practice and experience today, it is rare to find undue emphasis on life after death; what is stressed is the importance of caring for this world. Too great an emphasis on the coming of the messiah or on the world to come might tempt one to forget the challenges of this earth in which each individual is precious to God. Therefore, it is incumbent upon every person to address the turmoil and sufferings of the world in the day-to-day manner in which they present themselves and in the lives of ordinary people who come across one's path. As Harold Kushner explains, ". . . the danger of believing too fervently in a World to Come is that you may come to care less about the imperfections of this world. . . . If we love God, we should feel obliged to treat with love the world He loves so much. . . . The abstract concept of justice is meaningless unless it is translated into the lives of every citizen."[18]

In Jewish thought today, peoples' approaches to the topics of messiah, resurrection, and afterlife differ, ranging from the more literal and traditional to the more symbolic. The message of the teaching on resurrection emphasizes that human corporeal existence and striving to live ethically in the present flawed world in which we find ourselves are intrinsically precious to God. Life does not dissolve in futility and transience, for Jews hold that God is victorious over death. Rabbi Neil Gillman concludes that resurrection "affirms the significance of history and society, in which our embodied selves are located."[19] Far from thinking that life is purposeless or absurd, Judaism sees that humanity is called to have a relationship with God, who infuses his divine spirit into the souls of human beings. Death is not the end of that relationship, but the beginning of the reunification of the righteous with the Creator whose very nature is life giving and who invites humanity to act compassionately, mercifully, and righteously. The God who shows kindness and support throughout our lifetimes also grants the ultimate mercy—victory over the cruelty of death.

Notes

1. For additional biblical references see Isa 2:1-3, 42; 59:20; Jer 23:8; 30:3; Ezek 38:16; Hos 3:4-5; Mic 4:2-3; Zeph 3:9; Zech 14:9.

2. Chaim Pearl, *Theology in Rabbinic Stories* (Peabody MA: Hendrickson, 1997) 147.

3. In Ronald Isaacs, *Close Encounters: Jewish Views about God* (Northvale NJ and London: Jason Aronson, 1996) 117.

4. Leo Trepp, *Judaism: Development and Life*, 4th ed. (Belmont CA: Wadsworth, 2006) 286.

5. Quoted in Trepp, *Judaism*, 287.

6. Steven Katz, *The God I Believe In*, ed. Joshua Haberman (New York: The Free Press, 1994) 92.

7. Zalman Schachter-Shalomi, *Jewish with Feeling: A Guide to Meaningful Jewish Practice* (New York: Riverhead Books 2005) 224–27.

8. Steven S. Schwarzschild, "The Messianic Doctrine in Contemporary Jewish Thought," in *Concepts that Distinguish Judaism: God, Torah, Israel*, ed. Abraham Ezra Millgram (Washington DC: B'nai B'rith International, 1985) 252.

9. Ibid., 255–56.

10. Nissen Mangel, ed. and trans., *Siddur Tehillat Hashem* (New York: Merkos L'Inyonei Chinuch, 1982) 194.

11. Maurice Lamm, *The Jewish Way in Death and Mourning* (New York: Jonathan David Publishers, 1969) 231.

12. David S. Ariel cites *Tosefta Sanhedrin* 13:2 and *Mishneh Torah, Hilkhot Teshuvah* 3:5. See *What Do Jews Believe? The Spiritual Foundations of Judaism* (New York: Schocken, 1995) 229.

13. Jon Levenson, "The Resurrection of the Dead and the Construction of Personal Identity in Ancient Israel," in *Congress Volume: Basel 2001*, ed. A. Lemaire (Vetus Testamentum Supplements 92; Leiden: Brill, 2002) 308. Emphasis added.

14. Mangel, *Siddur*, 6–7.

15. Louis Jacobs, *The Book of Jewish Belief* (Springfield NJ: Behrman) 230.

16. David Wolpe, *The Healer of Shattered Hearts: A Jewish View of God* (New York: Henry Holt, 1990) 153–59.

17. Lamm, *The Jewish Way in Death and Mourning*, 232.

18. Harold Kushner, *To Life: A Celebration of Jewish Being and Thinking* (Boston and Toronto: Little, Brown) 44–45.

19. Neil Gillman, *Doing Jewish Theology: God, Torah and Israel in Modern Judaism* (Woodstock VT: Jewish Lights, 2008) 74.

Chapter 3

Revelation

Judaism holds that the One God, the author of all life, graciously reveals his will to humanity and commands all human beings to live an ethical life. The God who is Creator of all human beings is intimately involved in their lives. According to tradition, God unveiled the commandments that guide this universal morality to Adam and to Noah—in other words, to all of humankind. In addition, God designed a particular role for the Jewish people: to follow the torah as revealed to Moses. Thus, for Jews, the revelation of the torah at Sinai defines their mission as a people of the covenant. In this chapter, we turn first to the revelation that, as Judaism teaches, was given to all humanity, followed by an examination of key ideas of the revelation given to the Jewish people at Sinai.

Revelation for All Humankind

In Jewish thought, the entirety of God's creation is precious to him. Although God has a unique mission for the Jewish people—to guard and keep the torah—God also gives directives to all of humankind. These laws are known as the Noahide Commandments or the Seven Laws of Noah. By following these statutes, all can be judged righteous by God, and all can inherit a share in the world to come. While at first this may seem reductionist—that the torah contains 613 commandments for Jews (counted according to tradition) but only 7 for others—Judaism does not see it that way. Rather, the seven laws are key, capsule statements about how to relate to God and to relate to neighbor in every aspect of life, articulated in the form of commandments. They include directives regarding belief in God, relationships with one's fellow human beings, and the treatment of all creatures.

The Seven Laws of Noah—or principles of righteousness—are expressed as follows:[1]

1. *Belief in the one God.* This commandment teaches that God is the source of all that there is and that there is no power as his equal. It is noteworthy that Jewish teaching holds that beliefs and feelings (such as loving God) can

be commanded. This is so because actions that follow from beliefs can become habituated—and thus integrated into convictions. Belief in the one God has consequences: humanity is led to see that God is the author of morality and ethics. If there is one God, then people cannot select which commandments are required and which are optional.

Idolatry is defined as worshiping something other than the Creator, or denying the existence of God. In antiquity, the temptation was to believe in polytheistic systems. But even today, when worshiping other deities is not particularly compelling for most people, this commandment is still significant. Worshiping an idol is akin to putting one's own priorities, values, or excuses above the design, purpose, and justice demanded by the Creator. In other words, idolatry can be understood as worshiping the priorities set by one's own desires, urges, or personal struggles without regard to a nonnegotiable universal morality with God as its source. We might say that today's obsessions are often evident as self-indulgence, power, and greed at the expense of others; today's idolatry often puts materialism, accumulation, power, and wealth as the highest values one might pursue. In a non-idolatrous system, the standards for human behavior are transcendent; they come from God and are not relative.

The commandment of believing in one God also includes the directive that one not turn to any practices that claim to manipulate the future or see its outcome, such as necromancy, witchcraft, or other occult practices; believing in these powers is denying faith in God. The particular attraction of these idolatries is that they prey on desperate, suffering, and poor people. This first law of Noah not only proclaims the essential aspect of the connection between the one God, a universal morality, and a purposeful existence but also shows an empathetic concern for the extremes to which people will go in times of grief, serving to warn those who would take advantage of the unfortunate.

2. *Do not curse God.* The commandment not to curse God, or commit blasphemy, reminds humanity of the power of speech, which can change the world for either good or evil. Blasphemy is considered an attempt to drive out the divine presence or to deny God's existence; in effect, it annihilates God. In addition, anything that takes away from the reverence of God is considered a desecration of his name. Such actions are reckoned as demonstrating insufficient belief or incomplete faith in God as the Master of the Universe, the One who has a providential plan for all. The manner in which people respect God with their words also has consequences for the way their

fellow human beings are treated. By extension, then, this commandment teaches that it is imperative that people be careful with their speech regarding others, for insulting or reviling another person is tantamount to degrading the Divine.

3. *Do not murder.* It is no surprise that the universal laws of Noah include the prohibition not to murder, a law ingrained in the human heart for all persons of conscience. In Jewish teaching, this law, by extension, includes a prohibition against so-called mercy killings and suicide. Respect for life and its Author are so underscored that, for Jews, if one were threatened by another who said, "Kill this person or I shall kill you," one should rather give up his or her own life.

4. *Do not steal.* The commandment not to steal shows respect for property and for persons. It forbids not only the theft of goods but also the "theft of people" by kidnapping and sexual assault. In addition, this commandment shows respect for a person's right to earn a living and to be treated fairly in the work force; it prohibits gross overcharging and exacting unfair interest rates, and it insists that reliable weights and measures be used in commerce, demonstrating that everything comes from God—even one's livelihood. Practices associated with earning a living, therefore, must be upright, such as providing a salary, setting up honest business practices, or respecting the property and dwelling places of one's fellow human beings.

5. *Do not commit adultery or incest.* Respecting family is at the heart of the commandment that forbids certain sexual practices, such as committing adultery and incest. Although we might assume that committing incest is a natural taboo, this was not always the case. In the time of the second temple, for example, Jews were well familiar with the incestuous marriages in the royal families of their foreign rulers—an acceptable practice in the Hellenistic and Roman world. A sexual relationship is considered adulterous if the woman is married to another. Although modern people may be struck by the apparent lack of parity between men and women in this definition, it may make sense when we consider that the only way in which men can be certain of who their children are, and the only way in which anyone can be certain of the identity of his or her father (before DNA sampling!), is if a married woman has sexual relations exclusively with her husband.

6. *Do not eat the limb of a living animal.* The commandment to be kind to animals is stated in this seemingly strange way. It condemns not only what is expressed here literally—an apparently cruel and bizarre practice in antiquity—but also any inhumane slaughtering: one must be certain that animals

are dead before the first steps of meat processing begin. Although Judaism holds that God does not require vegetarianism, his sovereignty over creation must be acknowledged. No living thing is to be destroyed wantonly or cruelly. By extension, all living creatures are to be treated compassionately, and no aspect of nature is to be utilized without a legitimate purpose or a valid benefit.

7. *Set up just governments and a judicial system.* The Noahide Laws do not specify which type of government is just, but they insist that righteous authority and leadership be the hallmarks of the human community. Establishing a rule of law and a judicial system is essential in society so that people can exist with justice and peace. Within the context of this commandment, great emphasis is placed on the characteristics of honest, compassionate judges who have earned the respect of their communities before they hold court. They need to be God-fearing, acknowledging that all standards of justice come from a higher realm—from the justice of God, whom they serve.

Two additional commandments are often included in the Noahide Laws, namely, honoring parents and giving charity. Honoring parents not only embraces the concepts of deference and respect but also insists that (adult) children provide for their parents' basic needs of food, clothing, and shelter when they are unable to care for themselves. The commandment teaches not only that children are to treat parents with compassion but also that parents are to be forgiving, gentle, and kind to their children, whether they are trying to keep children on the right path or their children note a wrong that parents have done.

Judaism understands that the Noahide commandment to give charity reflects the kindness and mercy of God. As everything is ultimately a gift from the Creator, people must share graciously and compassionately with those in need. Both individuals and the community must see to it that the poor among them are provided for not only with monetary support but also with opportunities to obtain the skills to earn a living. This commandment is sensitive to the feelings of the poor as well as to the character of those who give because it emphasizes that one should provide assistance secretly, if possible, and that those who give are not to boast about their largesse.

Because it understands that God has a plan for all peoples and that there are different paths to the one, true God, Judaism is not a religion that proselytizes. There are particular commandments that are incumbent on the

Jewish people alone, but Judaism understands that all humans can choose good and avoid evil. These laws of Noah teach that all people can serve their Creator and each other in everyday acts of kindness, respect, and justice. They imagine a world in which humanity can see that the one God makes demands on everyone in order that creation can be filled with his presence.

Revelation for the Jewish People

If you had one way to love your beloved or 613 ways to love your beloved, which would you chose? Judaism holds that the 613 commandments given to the Jewish people at Mt. Sinai are far from being burdensome. Rather, they are 613 ways to be bound together with God. An individual commandment is called a *mitzvah* (plural *mitzvot*); when performing a *mitzvah* a person becomes connected with the Almighty. This is the reason God chose Israel: to receive and guard the torah, which contains all of God's teachings, instructions, and commandments (both ritual and ethical) given to the Jewish people. Accepting the torah at Sinai, the community agreed to obey the covenant God established with them. Sometimes, outside the Jewish world, the concept of being chosen is misunderstood. But in Judaism, God's reason for the choice of Israel is purposeful:

> For you are a people holy to the LORD your God; the LORD your God has chosen you out of all the peoples on earth to be his people, his treasured possession. It was not because you were more numerous than any other people that the LORD set his heart on you and chose you—for you were the fewest of all peoples. It was because the LORD loved you and kept the oath that he swore to your ancestors, that the LORD has brought you out with a mighty hand, and redeemed you from the house of slavery, from the hand of Pharaoh king of Egypt. (Deut 7:6-8)

Israel, "the fewest of all peoples," was elected because they agreed to accept the torah, whereas other nations did not. By continuing to accept and obey it, Israel attests to God's plan for the world. Maimonides underscores that, ultimately, the reason for following the commandments is love of God:

> Whoever serves God out of love, occupies himself with the study of the Law and the fulfillment of commandments and walks in the paths of wisdom, impelled by no external motive whatever, moved neither by fear of calamity nor by the desire to obtain material benefits; such a man does what is truly right because it is truly right, and ultimately happiness comes

to him as a result of his conduct. . . . When one loves God with the right
love, he will spontaneously observe all the commandments out of love.[2]

In Jewish teaching, the revelation at Sinai was composed of two types of
torah: the written torah and the oral torah. The written torah consists of the
five books of Moses (Genesis, Exodus, Leviticus, Numbers, and
Deuteronomy) and, by extension, may also refer to the entire Jewish Bible
(also known as the *Tanak*). But God also gave the oral torah at Sinai, namely,
all the interpretations of the written torah as well as principles of interpretation, which serve to address all aspects of life with God and with his creation.
These collections of the oral torah are found in extensive volumes known
collectively and informally as "the holy books." Chief collections include the
Mishnah and the Gomorrah (together the Mishnah and Gomorrah are
known as the Talmud), as well as the Midrashim. Each of these multivolume
works addresses how to act in the world, following God's teachings in everything one does.[3] In addition, the oral torah contains narratives that explain
gaps in Scripture or illustrate how to help one's fellow human beings, how to
enhance one's character, how to serve God, or how to live a holy life. The
genre of literature that details Jewish law is known as *halachah*, meaning "the
(proper) way to walk." The type of literature that instructs via narrative is
called *agaddah,* or "sayings." On the one hand, the oral torah can be considered a commentary on the written torah, but on the other hand, the oral
torah is much more. Besides its commentary on Scripture, it includes explanations regarding the history of tradition, teachings on loving God and
neighbor, and reflections on moral principles and individual character.

In order to review the vast subject matter of the torah, we briefly address
the organization of the Mishnah, which is divided into the following six categories: "seeds" is about agricultural laws in the land of Israel, sacrificial
offering to the priests and Levites, and contributions to the needy;
"appointed times" explains the practices and duties of keeping Shabbat and
festivals (religious holidays); "women" deals with family life, marriage, property, and divorce; "damages" is about person-to person relationships in the
areas of business, law courts, and criminal law, including "saving the victim
from his persecutor"[4]; "sacred things" details the laws relating to sacrifices in
the temple and dietary laws; and "purities" speaks about ritual purity and
impurity in the temple of old.[5]

In Jewish teaching, commandments can be between a person and God
or between one person and another. A commandment can tell you what to
do or what not to do; that is, it can be positive or negative. It can either

make rational sense or be inscrutable—its reason known only to God. Here we consider some examples of these (overlapping) categories. Positive commandments include belief in God, keeping Shabbat (the Sabbath day), saying prayers, visiting the sick, and giving charity. Negative commandments include prohibitions against stealing, owning fraudulent weights and measures (for business use), withholding an employee's wages, telling lies, and gossiping. Commandments that are considered rational include not stealing, not lying, not committing murder; commandments whose rationale are not understood include the dietary laws and sacrifices (in the days of the temple).[6]

In the following paragraphs, we consider examples from the collections of Jewish holy books. The first example shows how the Mishnah can provide a commentary on Scripture: Mishnah, *Seder Zeraim,* Tractate *Peah* Chapter 1/1 (translation: Mishnah; Order: "Seeds"; Essay on "The Corner of the Field"). Notice the four stages of this example.

Stage 1. This sample begins with a quotation from the book of Leviticus: "When you reap the harvest of your land, you shall not reap to the very edges of your field, or gather the gleanings of your harvest. You shall not strip your vineyard bare, or gather the fallen grapes of your vineyard; you shall leave them for the poor and the alien: I am the LORD your God" (Lev 19:9-10). Within the Bible, this passage is about the perimeters of any given agricultural field, giving instruction about the use of the boundaries of a defined plot. This *mitzvah,* known as the *peah* (literally, "corner"), says that farmers must not harvest the crops that are grown on the edges of their fields. These crops are to be left for the poor to gather for free.

Stage 2. With the biblical commandment quoted, the Mishnah next draws implications. Inspired by the care for the community that is discussed in Leviticus, it makes connections with other teachings (*mitzvot*). The passage continues, "These are the things that have no measure: The *peah* [corner] of the field, the first-fruits [given to the priest on the festival of Shavuot], the appearance [at the Temple in Jerusalem on Pilgrimage Festivals]; acts of kindness; and the study of the Torah." What does it mean to say that these things "have no measure"? It means that one should do them generously, without limit. If you are a farmer, you are to let the poor take whatever they need from the edges of your property. If it is the time of year to bring firstfruits to the priests, you give generously. Back in the time of the temple, if one were to ask, "How often should I come to Jerusalem for the appointed pilgrimage feasts?" the answer would be, "Every year (as long as you are physically able)!" Moreover, if one were to consider, "How many times must I be kind?" the answer would be, "To infinity!" "How much should I study torah?" "Ceaselessly!" Here we see that this Mishnah continues to make connections between the fruits, or harvest, of the land and the fruits, or consequences, of the *mitzvot*. The harvest of the corners of the field is thus linked with the effects that result from following the commandments.

Stage 3. Continuing with more examples of kindness, the Mishnah concludes that God sees all of these acts, rewarding the doers of good deeds in the World to Come (in eternity): "These are things the fruits of which a man enjoys in this world, while the principle remains for him in the World to Come: Honoring father and mother, acts of kindness, and bringing peace between a man and his fellow." Here you find that there are things so dear to God that their fruits, or effects, are felt both here, in this world, and in the World to Come.

Stage 4. The conclusion shows the extension of the significance of the passage: "But the study of Torah is equal to them all." With this ending we move from the corners of the field to other *mitzvot*, to the promise of eternal reward, and to the study of torah. How can it be that the study of torah is considered equal to magnanimous acts of self-sacrifice and kindness? Because, the oral torah teaches, if one studies these things, one will internalize them and perform the commandments automatically—they will be a part of the fabric of one's being and permeate everyday life. Daniel Feldman explains,

> The day to day interactions between people, the treatment of one another in mundane conversation, in walking in the street, in traveling on a bus, or waiting in line to be served in a store are no less the home of *halakhah* [Jewish law] than are the activities of the synagogue or the kitchen, the study hall or the hospital bed. Every form of relationship among men, not just monetary but personal as well, not just in the rabbinical court but also across the table at lunch, is the vital concern of Jewish law.[7]

The next example shows another way in which Scripture is used to illustrate important teachings. The following text shows how the Mishnah can reflect on many things that are important for living an ethical life and developing character. These statements appear as aphorisms, or maxims that use insights from Scripture. The Mishnah states, "Who is the wise one? He who learns from all men, as it says, 'I have acquired understanding from all my teachers' (Ps 119:99). Who is the mighty one? He who conquers his desire, as it says, 'slowness to anger is better than a mighty person'" (Prov 16:32). These teachings on humility, respect, patience, and self-discipline use the sayings of Scripture as a springboard for their declarations. The Mishnah continues, "Who is rich? He who is happy with his lot, as it is written (Ps 128:2) 'you shall eat the fruit of the labor of your hands; *you shall be happy, and it shall go well with you.*' '*You shall be*' refers to this world; and '*it shall go well with you*' refers to the world to come" (Mishnah, *Avot* 4:25).

This Mishnah demonstrates that each phrase of Scripture, which is of great consequence, can have application beyond its immediate biblical context. Every expression can be interpreted within the totality of Jewish teaching. This particular saying underscores that despite one's troubles, one can find joy in this life. Suffering is only temporary; God rewards the righteous in the World to Come.

The oral torah can also fill in the gaps of our knowledge that arise from what is found in the written torah, offering fuller explanations or detail. So, for example, in the collections of the Midrashim we find expansive detail of the lives of individuals who are encountered in the Bible, reasons why incidents occurred, connections between various events in Israel's history, and glimpses of the supernatural or World to Come. For example, in the biblical account of the Binding of Isaac (Gen 22), little is known of Isaac's speech or feelings. He asks only one question of his father Abraham: "The fire and the wood are here, but where is the lamb for a burnt-offering?" (Gen 22:7; *Genesis Rabbah* 56:4). The oral tradition deals with a host of issues in this compelling yet disturbing text. For example, why would God put Abraham to the test? The Midrash explains that although God knew of Abraham's faithfulness, the trial was given so that the whole world would understand why God chose Abraham to have a special role in his providential plan for humankind (*Genesis Rabbah* 56:7; 54:2). Throughout the journey up the mountain, Satan attempted to make Abraham renounce God and to have Isaac reject him as well. Thus, in the oral torah, we find that not only Abraham but also Isaac was personally tested, thereby becoming a paradigm of the martyr who submits to God's will. Sensitive to the troubling questions posed by this narrative, we find that the Midrash poignantly recounts Sarah's feelings as well. Misled by Satan, who tells the matriarch that Isaac was killed, Sarah dies of grief. These accounts that elaborate on Scripture do not give further information only for the sake of details. Rather, they illustrate the connectedness of all reality, exemplify model behavior, give encouragement in times of oppression and heartache, and offer ways to praise and thank God for blessings.

Maimonides prepared a list of the 613 *mitzvot*, gleaned from the Talmud and based on the written torah, succinctly listing the 248 positive and 365 negative commandments. The majority can no longer be practiced today because they apply to the temple sacrificial system or to the ancient theocratic state of Israel. Such commandments include laws that regulate the details of the daily sacrifices and those offered at the pilgrimage feasts, regulations for the activities of the priests who served at the temple, and duties of the king. Ritual and ethical laws do continue today, applying to business, agriculture, ritual and prayer, treatment of one's fellow human beings, and attitude toward God. We turn to the following examples from the diverse categories within Maimonides' lists: "imitate the just and upright ways of God"; "learn torah and teach it"; "circumcise males"; "pray to God"; "say grace after meals"; "do not stand idly by when a human life is at risk"; "do not put a stumbling block in front of another" (do not lead another into sin); "give charity according to one's means"; "love the stranger"; "honor father and mother"; "sanctify Shabbat"; "rejoice on (celebrate) the holidays"; "pay wages on time"; "make a fence around a roof" (to protect people from falling); and "return lost property." The diversity of these laws and their applicability to feelings and actions in both the private and public sectors show how torah truly affects all aspects of life.

To have an idea of how the practice of following the *mitzvot* in everyday life affects the lives of ordinary Jews, it is useful to look at the following commonly stressed acts of everyday kindness:[8]

1. *Give charity.* In English, the word "charity" comes from the Latin *caritas,* or love. In its root sense, therefore, the act of providing for the poor is connected with the act of love for one's fellow. But in Hebrew, there is a unique connotation of the word "charity." It comes from the Hebrew word "*tzedakah,*" meaning not love but rather justice or righteousness. Thus, in Jewish tradition, giving *tzedakah* is a duty commanded by God. To be sure, the act of giving is praiseworthy, but it does not come from one's largesse; rather, it is duty bound. In Jewish teaching, all that a person has is ultimately from God; thus, the obligation to give to others is ultimately not considered as deriving from one's own wealth—it is God's resource as well. The giver is simply dispersing it as God's partner. It is each person's responsibility to do so. Judaism teaches that while the act of giving charity is a duty, God sees and rewards this behavior, as is said in the book of Proverbs: "Whoever is kind to the poor lends to the LORD, and will be repaid in full" (Prov 19:17).

2. *Study torah.* One mark of a Jewish home is the presence and use of the holy books of the tradition. A basic set of traditional volumes would include

the following: a *siddur* (daily prayer book); the Five Books of Moses (*Chumash*) with commentary from the Midrash, Talmud, and words of selected sages throughout the centuries (from antiquity to the present); a collection of Psalms (*Tehillim*); a Bible (*Tanak*); the Talmud; the *Shulchan Aruch* (a guidebook for Jewish law); and other books on Jewish philosophy and daily living. The presence and use of these books contributes to an atmosphere that can inspire the members of the household to take the ideals and practices of their heritage to an implemented reality, encouraging members of the family to construct a meaningful life. Studying torah is not only a commandment; it is a way of life. In small and large ways, learning torah is integrated in the lives of children and adults. For young children, it might be learning prayers and doing projects pertaining to the holidays in religious school. For youth, it may be learning Talmud in a yeshiva. For adults, it may be weekly torah study classes on Shabbat afternoons. For others, it may consist of the occasional class, the reading of books, or the use of Jewish websites.

Torah study is considered a lifelong activity that can be done with a single friend or teacher, with a small group or a large class, daily or as time permits. Learning is done with the purpose not only of understanding God's teachings but also of incorporating them as one develops a relationship with the Almighty and with one's fellow human beings in all aspects of life: personally and professionally, in business and in family relationships, in exercising duty or in living friendships. The practice of contemplating, probing, and studying torah is a continuation of the centuries-old traditions of the sages who interpreted the Scriptures. It is considered a way to experience, question, and grow in understanding God's design for the world and for one's individual life.

3. *Pray.* Prayer is not only to be offered in times of difficulty or suffering but also is said in order to construct a daily connection with God, reminding each individual that the Author of life is the director of one's entire being. People not only ask God for help and guidance but also approach the Creator with thanksgiving and praise, thus forming the main way in which people allow their souls to approach the transcendent.

4. *Mark the doorposts of the home with* mezuzahs. A tangible reminder of God's presence in the home is found in what one sees. The *mezuzah*, the tiny scroll with verses from the prayer known as the *shema* (Hear, O Israel!), reminds the home's inhabitants of their connection with past generations and teachings as well as their ever-present relationship with God. The *mezuzah* stands as a concrete reminder of God's presence in the world.

5. *Light Shabbat candles.* An important ritual commandment that is stressed in Jewish living is lighting Shabbat candles. As sunset approaches on Friday evening, the women of the household light Shabbat candles, marking the holiness of this designated time (if there are no women in the household, men light Shabbat candles). The illumination symbolizes the peace and joy that is the spiritual mark of the day of rest, an aspect of existence that can permeate peoples' daily lives, even as they experience a material world. Keeping Shabbat begins with lighting candles on Friday at dusk, but it embraces much more. Other aspects include the prayer services of Friday night and Saturday day, hearing the torah readings, making *kiddush* (blessing over the wine), and having Shabbat meals. All of these practices emphasize community. Although it is possible to pray or have meals alone, it is not common practice. Shabbat is a time to gather with family and friends and to pray with the congregation in the synagogue.

6. *Put on* tefillin. A commandment incumbent upon Jewish males comes from the book of Deuteronomy: "Bind them [these words] as a sign on your hand, fix them as an emblem on your forehead" (Deut 6:8). This is the commandment of putting on *tefillin* (phylacteries). The biblical texts of Deuteronomy 6:4-9; 11:13-21; and Exodus 13:1-16 are written on parchment and placed in small boxes that men affix to the left arm and forehead for daily morning prayer. After bar mitzvah age (thirteen), Jewish men have this unique obligation. This practice reminds the one who prays that neither emotions nor intellect alone suffice in approaching God. One's mind (all one's intellectual faculties), one's heart (the entirety of one's feelings and emotions), and one's hands (all that one fashions) must be used in the service of God. The biblical verses found within the *tefillin* stress the unity of God and underscore that actions in this world have consequences, for there is eternal reward and punishment for the deeds of human beings. They declare the unity of God, recall the miracles of the past, and proclaim that God continues to be sovereign of the entire world. By wearing *tefillin* and by praying, Jews declare that they are willing to subject their own desires to God's will.

7. *Practice "acts of kindness."* Doing actions in which an individual specifically helps another is considered a crucially important commandment. Specific examples of committing one's life to doing these acts of kindness are given in the daily prayers: loaning money or other material goods, practicing hospitality, visiting and helping the sick, providing clothing for the poor, assisting brides and grooms, comforting mourners, burying the dead, and

helping to reconcile those who are fighting. Here is a reference to the importance of such acts found in the Talmud:

> Rabbi Hama son of Rabbi Hanina further said: What means the text: "You
> shall walk after God" (Deuteronomy 13)? . . . [The meaning is] to walk
> after the attributes of the Holy One. Just as God clothes the naked, as it
> says, "And God made garments of skins for Adam and his wife, and
> clothed them" (Genesis 3), so do you also clothe the naked. The Holy
> One, blessed be God, visited the sick, for it is written: "And God appeared
> to him by the oaks of Mamre" (Genesis 18), so do you also visit the sick.
> The Holy One, blessed be God, comforted mourners, for it is written:
> "And it came to pass after the death of Abraham, that God blessed Isaac his
> son" (Genesis 25), so do you also comfort mourners. The Holy One,
> blessed be God, buried the dead, for it is written: "And God buried him in
> the valley" (Deuteronomy 34), so do you also bury the dead. (Talmud,
> *Sotah* 14a)

The sages comment that in exercising these acts of kindness, one is emu-
lating the qualities of the Creator. Indeed, living a life according to torah
puts one on a quest for meaning and value in which one will walk along a
route guided by divine providence. Judaism teaches that when people are
conscious of keeping the *mitzvot*, their lives will be infused with meaning,
binding each person with God in a life of holiness—a life in which ideals are
put into action, thus helping to perfect the world.[9]

Ethical Living

Because Judaism holds that revelation teaches humanity the difference
between right and wrong through the commandments, its moral system
cannot be reduced to situational ethics. Ultimately, God determines morality. While it is true that circumstances change, the revelation of torah still
forms the basis on which to make all moral choices. Torah is seen as a divine
benchmark from which standards of behavior can be adjudicated. On a day-
to-day basis, as Jews go about business and participate in relationships, the
operative ethical axiom is this: because humanity is created in the image of
God, all must be treated with dignity and compassion. Everyday acts are to
be modeled on the attributes of God, who created humanity in his image.
The Talmud states, "Just as the Holy One, Blessed be He, is called
'Compassionate,' you should be compassionate; just as the Holy One,
Blessed be He, is called 'Gracious,' you should be gracious; just as the Holy

One, Blessed be He, is called 'Righteous,' you should be righteous; just as the Holy One, Blessed be He, is called 'Pious,' you should be pious."[10]

As Maimonides taught, the revelation of torah develops the character of both one's body and soul. Because of this, people learn to deal properly with one another and not do whatever one wants; torah enables one to see that acts must be in conformity with what is good for society. Thus, ethical quandaries must be deliberated within the context of "responsibilities, duties and obligations" that take precedence over "rights."[11] Moreover, Judaism teaches that individuals are not slaves or victims to their emotions. Although God defines what is right, humans have free will to choose the good and avoid evil.

Consider the example of Jewish teaching on the ethics of speech. The torah teaches that spreading gossip and defamation is forbidden. Maimonides clarifies that the torah prohibits "false witness, speaking falsehood, tale bearing, and cursing . . . obscene speech and slander."[12] In teaching the importance of this commandment for ethical living, Judaism underscores that communication is one of the characteristics that distinguishes human beings from the animals, coming from the very act of God breathing into humankind the "breath of life" (Gen 2:7). As Joseph Telushkin explains, "What we say about and to others can define them indelibly. That is why ethical speech—speaking fairly of others, honestly about ourselves, and carefully to everyone—is so important."[13]

Thus, it is part of Jewish tradition and teaching to guard one's statements, as words are seen to contribute to personality and one's emotional makeup. When dealing with others, the torah forbids that speech shame or embarrass people in public or that it be used to harm the reputation of others—even if the information is true. The only time unkind words can be spoken is when no other means are available to prevent harm or danger done to others. Being vigilant with one's speech allows people to emulate the Almighty as one is in partnership with him, transforming the world into a place that manifests God's goodness.

The Jewish teachings on the importance of the commandments—both those given to Moses and those given at Mt. Sinai—evidence the close bond that exists between the Revealer and humanity. On the often difficult paths of life in which humans find themselves, they are guided by God's instruction. When they fail, as all inevitably will, people can appeal to God for forgiveness and reconciliation. In his poem, "Hymn for Atonement Day," the medieval Jewish poet Yehuda HaLevi (1075–1141) captures the yearning of the Jewish heart that longs for God:

Lord, Your humble servants hear,
Suppliant now before You,
Our Father, from Your children's plea
Turn not, we implore You!

Lord, Your people, sore oppressed,
From the depths implore You;
Our Father, let us not, this day,
Cry in vain before You.

Lord, blot out our evil pride,
All our sins before You;
Our Father, for Your Mercy's sake,
Pardon, we implore You.

Lord, no sacrifice we bring,
Prayers and tears implore You;
Our Father, take the gift we lay,
Contrite hearts, before You.

Lord, Your sheep have wandered far,
Gather them before You;
Our Father, let Your shepherd love
Guide us, we implore You.

Lord, Your pardon grant to all
That in truth, implore You;
Our Father, let our evening prayer
Now find grace before You.

Lord, Your humble servants hear,
Suppliant now before You;
Our Father, from Your children's plea
Turn not, we implore You![14]

Notes

1. For further information, see Chaim Clorfene and Yakov Rogalsky, *The Path of the Righteous Gentile: Introduction to the Seven Laws of The Children of Noah* (Southfield MI: Targum Press, 1987).

2. Avraham Berkovitz, trans. and ed., *Pearls of the Rambam: Maimonides; Commentary on the Torah, Numbers, Deuteronomy* (Jerusalem: Mosad Harav Kook, 2007) 2:771.

3. See further, Joel Roth, "Seeking the Reasons for the Mitzvot: Pros and Cons," *Conservative Judaism* 61/3 (Spring 2010): 3–11.

4. Adin Steinsaltz, *The Essential Talmud: Thirtieth Anniversary Edition*, trans. Chaya Galai (New York: Basic Books, 2006) 110.

5. Ibid., 109–11.

6. Louis Jacobs, *The Book of Jewish Belief* (Springfield NJ: Behrman, 1984) 29–37.

7. Daniel Z. Feldman, *The Right and the Good: Halakah and Human Relations* (New York: Yashar Books, 2005) xii.

8. See for example, the website, "Ten Absurdly Simple Ways to Live Higher," from Chabad, a Jewish outreach organization that encourages integration of Jewish life into daily experience; online at http://www.chabad.org/library/howto/wizard_cdo/aid/142434/jewish/Introduction.htm (accessed 11 June 2012).

9. Reuven Hammer, "Judaism as a System of Mitzvot," *Conservative Judaism* 61/3 (Spring 2010): 23. See further, pp. 12–25.

10. *Sifrei, Eikev*, as quoted in Moshe Miller and Eli Silberstein, *Talmudic Ethics: Timeless Wisdom for Timely Dilemmas* (New York: Merkos L'Inyonei Chinuch, n.d.) 17.

11. Ibid., 20–21.

12. Commentary on Mishnah *Avot*, ch. 1, quoted in Miller and Silberstein, *Talmudic Ethics*, 57.

13. Joseph Telushkin, *Words That Hurt, Words That Heal: How to Choose Words Wisely and Well* (New York: Quill William Morrow, 1996), 4–5.

14. "The Poetry and Prose of Yehudah ha-Levi," http://www.inspirationalstories.com/poems/hymn-for-atonement-day-yehudah-halevi-poems (accessed 5 June 2012).

Chapter 4

The Jewish People

Some groups of people feel a connection with each other on account of their common origins and experiences, and others sense it because of their religious practices. Jews see themselves as being connected by their shared history, culture, ethnicity, and religious tradition. It is impossible to extract only one of these.[1] By (Orthodox) Jewish law, a Jew is defined as one who is born of a Jewish mother or who converts to Judaism according to Jewish law (*halacha*). Reform Judaism also accepts as Jews children of Jewish fathers if they have been raised Jewish. Whether one is born a Jew or converts to Judaism, one is considered a child of Abraham and Sarah. The torah teaches that the soul of every Jewish person was present at Mt. Sinai, for the commandments were given by God and were made not only with the people standing there but also with Jews of every generation. Perhaps this is key for understanding why one cannot choose whether Jews are bound either ethnically or through faith. All Jews are considered part of the family of Abraham and Sarah; all are connected both by the promise God made to the ancestors and by the covenant revealed at Sinai. In the modern world, in which many people do not feel a strong attachment to any faith, there are many Jews who—although not religious in a traditional sense—feel a strong Jewish identity that is centered on people, culture, and tradition. Others strive to keep all religious practices as well as customs and traditions; still others keep many but not all aspects of Shabbat and holidays.

Because Jews have been scattered throughout the diaspora (the lands outside Israel), differences in customs, languages, and traditions have arisen throughout the globe. Jews are characterized today by two main subdivisions of ethnicity and culture: Ashkenazim and Sephardim, with a number of additional smaller groups, such as Ethiopian, Indian, and central Asian. Ashkenazim trace their roots to northern and eastern Europe; Sephardim to Spain, North Africa, and the Middle East. Sephardim and Ashkenazim share the same collections of holy books but have some different customs in such areas as liturgical and holiday practices. One portion of the Sephardim traces customs to the period of diaspora life in the Iberian Peninsula, followed by settlement in North African communities after their expulsion from Spain that occurred in 1492. The Sephardim who originate from the Middle Eastern nations of Iran, Iraq, and Yemen have ancestry in those lands that may be traced back to the Babylonian exile of the sixth century BCE. Nearly all Jews from North Africa and the Middle East emigrated or were evacuated to the state of Israel after 1948, as conditions in their communities grew violent and dangerous after the creation of the modern state. The Ashkenazi Jewish community is found today in the Americas, Europe, Australia, South Africa, and Israel (the majority of American Jews are of Ashkenazi descendant). Ethiopian Jews were isolated from the rest of the Jewish world for thousands of years, and until recent decades they were unaware of the development of the oral torah. Thus, they have a far greater number of unique practices. The majority of Ethiopian Jews were clandestinely rescued from the oppressive regime of their country in the 1980s and 1990s and airlifted to Israel.

Besides being linked by the covenant with Abraham, Jews are joined together by the covenant at Sinai and the covenant with David. The torah given at Sinai forged a bond, as many of the commandments are concerned with community: they explain how to keep Shabbat and holidays; how to support one another in education, business, and charity; how to follow life-cycle events of birth, marriage, and mourning; and how to foster good family relations and peace in the home. The covenant with David binds the Jewish people with each other as well as with all human beings because from the promise to David comes hope for the final redemption: the coming of the messiah and the perfection of the world. We now turn to these fundamental aspects of daily life that help to define what it means to live as a Jew.

Prayer

Even before the destruction of the second temple by the Romans, the role of prayer and the place of the synagogue were important in Jewish life. But from the time of the second temple's destruction, they became even more significant. Instead of sacrifice and temple worship in the holiest of locations, every day was made distinctive—holy—by observing the commandments, celebrating Shabbat and the holidays, and participating in life-cycle events. These acts, performed both at home and in the synagogue either individually or communally, are marked by blessings and prayer.

Prayer is seen as a means to draw people closer to God. In Hebrew, the word for prayer is *tefillah*; it comes from the root word meaning "to judge oneself." In examining themselves, individuals consider their relationship to God and their purpose in life while opening up their hearts to God. As Jews believe in personal divine providence, prayer is not only a time to thank and praise God but also an occasion to engage in personal introspection and petition. One asks, "What is my role in life at this time and in this place? How does God want me to help my family and community? What can I do to make the world a better dwelling place for God? How do I endure my current problems or sorrow? What areas of my life do I need to change? Where have I missed the mark in doing God's commandments? For which acts do I need to ask God for forgiveness? In which areas of my life do I need God's help?" Prayer can fundamentally change peoples' outlooks about their situation. Despite the gulf that exists between God and humanity, Judaism teaches that with prayer, one can truly approach the transcendent. In prayer, "one approaches God despite the inadequacies in one's personality, despite the inadequacy of language, despite the inadequacy of what we can offer God."[2] The prayers of the *siddur* (the Jewish prayer book), compiled between the first and sixth centuries CE, are designed to aid in these goals.[3]

In Jewish practice, we find the following kinds of prayers: thanksgiving, praise, confession, petition, and introspection. Prayers can be either individual or communal and said in the home, synagogue, or other community places. In Orthodox Jewish practice, daily services are offered in the morning, afternoon, and evening. The afternoon and evening services are combined (said at twilight) so that, in effect, daily synagogue prayer is offered twice a day. Praying in community reminds one to reach out in love with one's fellow and to stand in solidarity with the community, ready to assist, to care, and to motivate each other in service of God, with responsibility shown to one another.

Examples of individual prayers include those said when rising in the morning, before bedtime, before and after meals, for safety in traveling, for thanksgiving when being saved from danger, or when witnessing great phenomena (such as seeing a rainbow, viewing lightning, observing the path of a comet). In addition, blessings are said before performing certain commandments (such as lighting Shabbat candles or placing a mezuzah on the doorpost of one's home) or when hearing of the good fortune of others, such as when someone is blessed with a child. These blessings elevate the community's observations of the awe-inspiring aspects of the acts of the Creator and link the community in joy with the appreciation of God's blessings. As Marcia Falk remarks, blessings are the "heart and soul" of Jewish prayer: "A blessing—in Hebrew, *berakhah*—is an event; a blessing is also that which

turns a moment *into* an event. Blessings intensify life by focusing our attention on our actions, increasing our awareness of the present moment."[4]
There is even a blessing for when one receives bad news. For example, upon
hearing of the death of a loved one, the response is, "Blessed is the True
Judge." The idea here does not, to be sure, solve the problem of theodicy
(God's justice, namely, how can a good God allow evil and suffering?), but
such a blessing does demonstrate the way in which faith addresses the problem. In Judaism, the mysterious ways of God are not known. It is believed,
however, that in an inscrutable way, everything serves a purpose in the divine
plan, even when we cannot see it. The Jewish scholar Reuven Grodner
writes,

> . . . the human being has no way of understanding how God keeps His bal-
> ance sheets. He must resign himself to faith in the Supreme Judge. The
> faithful Jew believes that the reward of the wicked is merely temporal,
> whereas the reward of the righteous is eternal. . . . Promises of reward for
> observing mitzvot are not meant for this world. They are meant for the
> World to Come.[5]

We will examine some well-known blessings—the short prayers that permeate Jewish life. These prayers, as a whole, elevate Jews' entire existence,
connecting them with the Source of all life and blessing. They thank God
for the gifts of nature, food, health, and other good things; praise him
for the blessings of everyday life; and acknowledge the requirement of performing various commandments. Examples include the morning blessings
said on arising, such as, "Blessed are you, O Lord our God, who restores my
soul. . . . Blessed are you, O Lord our God, King of the Universe, who heals
the sick." They include statements of gratitude for the food that sustains life
itself: "Blessed are you, O Lord our God, King of the universe, who creates
the fruit of the tree." They acknowledge acts of dedication, such as the blessing said before the lighting of Shabbat candles: "Blessed are you, O Lord our
God, king of the universe, who sanctifies us and commands us to light the
Shabbat candles." Blessings recognize that God is king and the giver of commandments; he sustains life, gives the pleasures of food and drink, delivers
people from danger, and brings his creation to special occasions of joy.
Blessings confirm that the world is God's alone and that his creation enjoys
everything in it by divine decree, as his gifts. In fact, in Jewish thought the
chasm between the sacred and profane is not stressed because everything in

the physical, material world can be sacred, sanctified, set apart for God's purpose.

The best-known prayer in Judaism is the *shema,* considered the watchword of Israel's faith. This prayer is said individually in the morning blessings and before bed at night and also in daily and Shabbat services.

> Hear O Israel, the LORD is our God, the LORD is One. You shall love the LORD your God with all your heart, with all your soul, and with all your might. And these words which I command you today shall be in your heart. You shall teach them thoroughly to your children, and you shall speak of them when you walk on the road, when you lie down and when you rise. You shall bind them as a sign on your hand, and they shall be for a reminder between your eyes. And you shall write them upon the doorposts of your house and upon your gates.[6]

Note how the love of God, faith in him, and willingness to do the commandments form the essence of this biblical prayer. In addition, the importance of passing on the faith and practice of Judaism to the next generation is underscored. The recitation of the *shema* also includes various blessings. Here are examples:

> Blessed are You, Lord our God, King of the universe who forms light and creates darkness, who makes peace and creates all things. In mercy He gives light to the earth and to those who dwell thereon, and in His goodness He renews each day, continuously, the work of Creation . . . God of the universe, in Your abounding mercies have compassion on us . . . Be blessed, Lord our God, in the heavens above and on the earth below . . . Enlighten our eyes in Your Torah, cause our hearts to cleave to Your commandments, and unite our hearts to love and fear Your Name . . . May we rejoice and exult in Your salvation. Lord our God, may Your mercy and Your abounding kindness never, never forsake us.[7]

Throughout these blessings, God the Creator is seen as one who is still intimately connected with his creation. He is far from a God who created the world once and then forgot or abandoned it. Similarly, the God who redeemed Israel once in time continues his presence among the Jewish people and among all human beings.

The prayer that forms a key part of the daily as well as the Shabbat services is known as "The Eighteen Benedictions" (the *Shemone Esrei* or *Amidah*). This prayer includes both praise and supplications.

You are holy and Your Name is holy, and holy beings praise you daily for all eternity . . . . Graciously bestow upon us from You, wisdom, understanding, and knowledge . . . . Cause us to return, our Father, to Your torah; draw us near, our King, to Your service; and bring us back to You in whole-hearted repentance . . . . Pardon us, our Father, for we have sinned: forgive us, our King, for we have transgressed; for You are a good and forgiving God . . . . Heal us, O Lord, and we will be healed; help us and we will be saved . . . . Bless us, Lord our God, this year and all the varieties of its produce for good . . . . We will give thanks to You and recount Your praise, evening, morning and noon, for our lives which are committed into Your hand, for our souls which are entrusted to You, for Your miracles which are with us daily, and for Your continual wonders and beneficences. . . . For by the light of Your countenance You gave us, Lord our God, the Torah of life and loving-kindness, righteousness, blessing, mercy, life and peace . . . . Blessed are You Lord, who blesses His people Israel with peace.[8]

These words evidence the attitude cultivated by Jewish life: to see the world as full of God's blessings and goodness. It is a world filled with daily blessings and miracles—as long as one is willing to see them.

This sampling of prayers gives an indication of the daily connections made between the individual and the community with God. Jewish thought sees God and his creation as worthy of praise and thanksgiving. It believes that God is compassionate, loving, and forgiving. He accepts petitions and hears the cries of those who suffer.

Life-cycle Events

The Jewish community is a close-knit, warm, and welcoming group that cares for each other. This connection with each other is reflected in the life-cycle events that begin the Shabbat after a baby's birth up until the time of a person's death.

Circumcision (*Bris/Berit Millah*)

Because being Jewish is both being a member of a people and being part of a faith, a child is considered to be a Jew from the moment he or she is born. All Jewish boys are included in the covenant of circumcision eight days after their birth (but remain Jews even if they never experience this rite). The covenant of circumcision is not only for the child, whose Jewish identity is celebrated, but also for the entire community, who welcome another gift from God into their midst. For the child, the significance, to be sure, becomes known only when he grows up. Harold Kushner remarks that the full significance only becomes apparent when he does the same for his own son, for "a Jew is born into the Covenant with God whether he wants to be or not, and this Covenant involves pain and sacrifice as well as honor and sanctity. . . . The Covenant can be violated; it cannot be escaped. It is part of who you are, branded into your flesh at birth."[9] The ceremony itself usually takes place at the home or synagogue. Two people are given unique roles of privilege in the ceremony and take responsibility to be special figures in the child's life: the godfather, who holds the child during the circumcision, and the godmother, who carries the child into the room. A special seat of honor is placed near the child, although it remains empty. This chair is symbolically reserved for Elijah, who, according to tradition, sustains the Jewish people. At the *bris* (also known as the *berit millah*—the covenant of circumcision), the father recites this blessing: "Blessed are You, O Lord our God . . . who has commanded us to initiate him into the covenant of our Father Abraham."[10] The congregation expresses its hope that the child become learned in torah, be a keeper of the commandments, and be blessed with marriage: "as he has entered the covenant, so may he enter into Torah, marriage, and good deeds." Ending the ceremony, the child receives his name with these words: "Our God and God of our Fathers: preserve this child unto his father and mother, and may his name in Israel be called: *Proper Name, son of Name of Father.*" In Jewish life today, many children have Hebrew or Yiddish given names, used for both secular (or legal) and religious purposes (Yiddish is a European [Germanic] language of Ashkenazi Jewry, written with the Hebrew alphabet). Other families, however, have the practice of giving a child a name from any language but reserve a special Hebrew (or Yiddish) name for him or her as well, used on ceremonial occasions. This Hebrew name is the one by which the person is known during all Jewish rituals—it is the name by which one is called to read the torah, invoked in personal prayer, said in the marriage ceremony, and written on the Jewish wedding contract. It is customary in Ashkenazi circles to name the child after a deceased relative and, in Sephardi communities, to name the child after a beloved living relative. The naming not only honors the namesake and links the generations but also expresses the hope that the child will live according to the good deeds of the one whose name he or she bears.

Although the circumcision ceremony is incumbent on boys alone, baby girls are welcomed into the community as well. In Orthodox congregations, at the first Shabbat after the child's birth, the family is honored with prayers, blessings, the naming of the baby, and celebration. In Reform congregations in recent decades, a baby naming ceremony for girls has been developed. In this ceremony, the parents together recite this blessing: "Blessed are You . . . who has commanded us to sanctify life . . . who has granted us life, sustained us, and enabled us to reach this occasion."

Bar/Bat Mitzvah

As a child is growing up, it is considered the parents' responsibility to ensure that he or she follows the *mitzvot*. However, when a boy reaches age thirteen, and when a girl reaches twelve (thirteen in Reform congregations), he or she is considered old enough to take individual responsibility for the commandments (the year difference for the genders recognizes that girls mature earlier than boys). The ceremonies of *bar mitzvah* and *bat mitzvah* (meaning "son of the covenant" and "daughter of the covenant," respectively) mark this important occasion. Often portrayed inaccurately in television and in movies, the most important parts of this occasion are the preparation and the religious ceremony itself, which consist of learning how to lead prayers, reading from the torah, and doing other good deeds. Boys in Orthodox congregations, and both boys and girls in Reform and Conservative synagogues, lead the community in prayer and read from the torah during Shabbat services. Many children volunteer in outreach programs while they prepare for their ceremony, such as working with the elderly or disabled, helping with young children, and assisting with other opportunities in the synagogue. To be sure, social gatherings and parties may follow the religious ceremony. But the point of such celebration is to mark that the child who has become *bar* or *bat mitzvah* has achieved a basic knowledge of the essence of Jewish beliefs and practice, gained familiarity with the Hebrew language of prayer and Scripture, and takes his or her stand as a link in the chain of an ancient people and their traditions.

Marriage

In Jewish life, marriage is considered a union of two souls in which the husband and wife complete each other in their shared goals, coming together under the canopy of God's presence. Within Jewish tradition, love and intimacy are celebrated in the context of marriage in which two become united as one soul. Nonetheless, one's individuality is not subsumed in marriage; rather, in marriage there is "the joining of equals, a mutuality, a reciprocal love."[11] In the context of marriage and loving companionship, a family is born, a place in which its members learn to love and care for one another. It can be a place for God to dwell. Although not the only reason for marriage, being open to having children is considered a religious obligation in Judaism.

The time before the ceremony is considered a period to become close to God; the couple fasts in accordance with the propitious time for God to forgive sins. Before the ceremony, the bride, groom, and witnesses gather to sign the *ketubah,* the traditional wedding contract that enumerates the obligations of the couple to one another. Often, a *ketubah* is beautifully decorated, serving as artwork for the couple's home. Before the two gather together for the ceremony, the groom veils the bride, a tradition that is linked with the biblical account of Rebekah's modesty when greeting her betrothed, Isaac (Gen 24:65). In Orthodox tradition, the groom enters the wedding canopy—the *chuppah*—accompanied by his father and the bride's father; the bride enters accompanied by her mother and the groom's mother. In Reform congregations, the bride and groom are each accompanied by their parents. The *chuppah,* a cloth held by four poles, or a stationary decorative structure, epitomizes the new home of the couple; its open sides are symbolic of the newlyweds' home as a welcoming, inviting place. Some couples have the custom of having the bride circle the groom seven times, representing that the wife enters "into the very core of her husband's soul," and to symbolically incorporate the prophet Jeremiah's adage concerning the joy to be experienced by returning exiles: "a woman encompasses a man" (Jer 31:22).[12] Gathered with the couple under the *chuppah,* the rabbi says words of welcome and blessing. After the bride and groom have drunk from the same cup of wine, the groom places the ring on the index finger of the bride's hand with these words: "May you be sanctified to me with this ring, according to laws of Moses and Israel." (Later the bride transfers the band to her ring finger.) Seven blessings are offered in the presence of the couple— blessings that thank God for his creation of the universe and of humanity in his image "in such fashion that they in turn can create life," for the restoration of Zion, and for the joy of the bride and groom.[13] The prayers express that the bride and groom participate in the happiness that only God can give, a joy that will fully be realized at the time of the final redemption. Hence, the groom breaks a glass in memory of the destruction of the temple and in anticipation of God's promise to restore Zion and to grant salvation. (Typically, the glass is wrapped in a cloth and the groom crushes it with his foot.) Thus, even in times of greatest exultation, the context of the history of the people—their sufferings and their hopes—are brought to memory.

Death

When death occurs, there is a Jewish way of mourning and burial as well. Cremation, embalming, and autopsies are considered disrespectful to the body (exceptions are made in some circumstances, as when complying with governmental stipulations in case of suspected murder). There is no wake to show the body of the deceased in Jewish tradition. Because people are made in the image of God, it is considered disrespectful to delay burial or to invade the body with embalming procedures that disguise the loss. The body of the deceased is washed (a sign of purification) by trained volunteers who show great respect, not even speaking while doing this act of kindness that can never be repaid. From the time of death until burial, the body is never left unattended. Those who stand watch offer prayers and recite psalms (commonly Psalms 23 and 91).

Burial normally takes place within twenty-four hours. At the funeral service, prayers are offered and a eulogy is usually given. At the interment site, the rabbi and mourners say prayers and participate in the burial. Everyone puts a spade of earth into the burial ground, but it is customarily done by using the shovel with its blade turned backwards to mark the sanctity of what is being done; this is not an ordinary task. The grave is completely filled by the loved one's friends and family. Families abide by the tradition that extends back to biblical days of tearing their garments, symbolizing the breaking of their hearts from the profound loss (this is sometimes done by simply wearing a torn ribbon pinned to one's clothing.) This particular practice is done by the closest of relations: father, mother, brother, sister, son, daughter, or spouse. The following prayer for the deceased captures the essence of the service:

> O God, full of compassion, who dwells on high, grant true rest upon the wings of the *Shechinah* [divine presence], in the exalted spheres of the holy and pure, who shine as the resplendence of the firmament, to the soul of [the name of the deceased] who has gone to his [supernal] world, for charity has been donated in remembrance of his soul; may his place of rest be in *Gan Eden* [the World to Come]. Therefore, may the All-Merciful One shelter him with the cover of His wings forever, and bind his soul in the bond of life. The Lord is his heritage; may he rest in his resting-place in peace.[14]

After the burial, families begin the week of sitting *shiva*—the seven-day mourning period—in which family and friends gather to pray and offer condolences in the home of the bereft. Just as God offers solace to the mourners, so too is it an obligation for the community to comfort those who reach the depths of loneliness in this intensely sad time. It is not customary to send flowers; rather, donations to charity in the person's name are considered a way to honor the deceased. Throughout the week of *shiva*, the closest relations sit on low chairs as an indication of their grief and in consonance with the ancient practice of sitting on the ground while in mourning. There are certain customs done by the closest family members listed above. Throughout either eleven or twelve months after the death (depending on custom) of the loved one, the well-known prayer, the Mourner's *Kaddish*, is recited by the bereaved. Because of the belief in the continuation of the soul after death, Judaism teaches that one can pray for the departed. Its basic theme is the sanctification of God's name:

> Exalted and hallowed be His great Name throughout the world which He has created according to His will. May He establish His kingship, bring forth His redemption and hasten the coming of His Mashiach [messiah] in your lifetime and in the lifetime of the entire House of Israel, speedily and soon. . . . May His great name be blessed forever and to all eternity. Blessed and praised, glorified, exalted and extolled, honored, adored and lauded by the Name of the Holy One, blessed be He, beyond all the blessings, hymns, praises and consolations that are uttered in the world. . . . He who makes peace in His heavens, may He make peace for us and for all Israel.[15]

For all that is unknown after death, this prayer publicly proclaims that God designed the world for good and that the human task is to work alongside God as partners to make it worthy as a home for God's presence.

Yahrzeit

The *yahrzeit* refers to the anniversary of a loved one's death. Throughout the year, deceased family relations are remembered on the anniversary of the date of death (as determined by the Jewish calendar), on Yom Kippur, and on the festivals of Sukkot (Booths), Pesach (Passover), and Shavuot (Weeks) (the three pilgrimage holidays of the times of the first and second temples). A portion of each of these holiday services is devoted to memory of the loved ones; mourners recite *kaddish* and pledge charity in memory of the deceased. The *kaddish*, said publicly with a *minyan* (a quorum of ten), calls on the faithful to remember God's holiness. Relatives light a memorial candle (that burns for twenty-four hours) and may mark the date of the anniversary with special prayers, torah study, and a visit to the gravesite—accompanied with this prayer: "May it be Your will that the rest of this departed be with honor, and his or her merit stand up for me."[16] It is customary that those visiting the grave mark it with a small sign of their presence—a tiny stone or pebble that evidences the respect given to the deceased.

Everyday Jewish Life

Signs, symbols, and customs of Jewish life not only occur in prayer, holiday celebration, and life-cycle events but also in everyday Jewish life that is filled with tangible reminders of Jewish teachings and values. The physicality of the familiar world is infused with reminders of God's presence that touch the senses. With these holy objects, such as the *tallit, tefillin,* and the *mezuzah,* Jews bring together the spiritual and the material in order to make *this world* a dwelling place for God. In addition, there are customary (secular or ordinary) objects that are quite familiar in Jewish life. First, we turn to important examples that are considered holy—designated for a particular purpose.

The *Mezuzah*

The *mezuzah* is a small piece of parchment inscribed with the *shema,* i.e., the biblical passages Deuteronomy 6:4-9 and 11:13-21. We examined the first part of the *shema* above. Here is its continuation, found in the *mezuzah:*

> Therefore place these words of mine upon your heart and upon your soul, and bind them for a sign on your hand, and they shall be for a reminder between your eyes . . . so that your days and the days of your children may be prolonged on the land which the Lord swore to your fathers to give to them for as long as the heavens are above the earth.[17]

These words underscore the uniqueness of God, the requirement of allegiance to his teachings, the importance of handing on the tradition to the next generation, and the blessings that come from living according to the divine plan. The magnitude of these words is sometimes enhanced by the practice of encasing the scroll in beautiful containers that can reflect many styles of artistic expression. The outside of the tiny scroll is marked with the Hebrew word *Shaddai* ("The Almighty"). Rolled up, it is affixed to doorposts, serving as a constant reminder of one's obligations to God and showing the connection between the spiritual and material worlds, bringing people closer to God.

Just as the *mezuzah* brings to mind the importance of the *shema* to all who enter the home or other buildings, so too do *tefillin* (phylacteries) serve a similar function. *Tefillin* are small boxes that contain tiny scrolls with the words of the *shema*. One is attached with leather straps to the left arm and the other to the forehead during weekday morning prayers; this practice is typically followed by Orthodox and Conservative Jewish men.

Tallit

In Jewish practice, the *tallit* (or *tallis*), a garment with fringes, is used in prayer as a physical reminder of the commandments and as a marker of identity. As is found in the Bible, Jewish men are commanded to wear a four-cornered garment with fringes (Num 15:38; Deut 22:12). There are two kinds: the large *tallit* (*tallit gadol*), which is worn during morning prayer, and the small *tallit* (*tallit katan*), which observant Jewish males wear at all times, along with their regular clothing. On the *tallit* one finds the *tzitzit* (fringes), a tangible reminder of the commandments. Although not commanded to do so, some women in the Conservative and Reform traditions have adopted the practice of wearing the *tallit* while praying. When donning this garment, one says this prayer: "The children of men take refuge in the shadow of Your wings. . . . Bestow Your kindness upon those who know You, and Your righteousness on the upright in heart."[18] The *tallit* can also be used as a wedding canopy (*chuppah*) when held above the couple during the ceremony.

Yarmulke/kippah

The yarmulke or kippah is a small skullcap worn by Jewish men (and some Jewish women) during prayer. Although some Reform Jews have the custom of not necessarily wearing a yarmulke during services, by and large it is considered a necessary sign of respect to God for Jewish men to don it during prayer. Wearing a kippah at all times is more customary than required, but in common practice, most Orthodox Jewish men will wear one at all times as a sign of living by the commandments.

Synagogue

In biblical times, both sacrifice and prayer were the main avenues to approach God. After the destruction of the Second Temple (in 70 CE), sacrifice was no longer a possibility. Thus, the synagogue became more important and more common. The synagogue is known as a House of Prayer, a House of Assembly, and a House of Study.[19] Besides a building for holding services, a synagogue is also a community and a learning center. Thus, people gather to study torah and traditions with the rabbi or with other teachers, organize philanthropic activities and social action, and draw together informally. Synagogues are congenial places that have social activities for all ages. Reform congregations usually call a synagogue a "temple"; Orthodox synagogues may call it a "*shul*," (the Yiddish word for synagogue). In all branches of Judaism, synagogues may be either humble rooms or expansive buildings.

A central defining aspect of a synagogue is the *bimah*, an elevated platform for the reading of the torah scroll. Torah scrolls are housed in an ark, usually a wooden structure (cabinet) covered with an embroidered curtain— a traditional reminder of the ark of the covenant, the wooden chest that held the tablets of the law from the time of Moses. The ark is placed on the wall that faces Jerusalem, the site of the former holy temple. Near the ark is placed the eternal light—an oil lamp or candle—that is lit before services, a symbol of God's guiding presence in the world and within the congregation. Its history goes back to the usage of the menorah, or seven-branched oil lamp, which was used in the sanctuary and later in the temple. It is significant that Judaism teaches that a synagogue must have windows, as they symbolize that one's prayers and good deeds must go out into the world.

Star of David, *Chamsa*, and *Chai*

Other symbols commonly used in Jewish art and culture that are found within the synagogue and within the home, in jewelry, or in other visuals are the *magen David* (the Star of David), the menorah (lampstand/candelabra), the c*hamsa* (a hand with a jeweled eye in the center), and the *chai* (a two-letter Hebrew word meaning "life"). Except for the menorah, whose prototype was used in the ancient temple of Jerusalem, it is difficult to trace the origins of these symbols. The Star of David has been linked with the shield of King David in popular imagination; from the time of the twentieth century it has become widespread as a Jewish symbol and is found on the Israeli flag. The *chamsa* is found cross-culturally in the Middle East and has been historically associated with protection against "the evil eye" (anything harmful). The *chai*, often used in jewelry, consists of the Hebrew letters *het* and *yod* that spell the word "life"—the same word used in the toast or tribute: "*l'chaim*"—to life! Here is the way "*chai*"appears in Hebrew letters: חי.

Minyan

A *minyan* (quorum) of ten is required for many prayers and for reading the torah portion. In Jewish thought, it is understood that the *shekinah* (the divine presence) dwells among the assembly gathered for prayer. Prayers are said in the name of the entire community, and there is a special feeling of focus and meditation within the group as individuals reinforce each other when addressing their prayers to God. The torah readings are divided into fifty-four weekly portions (*sidras* or *parshas*). It takes a full year to read the torah (the first five books of the Bible) in the synagogue. Each shabbat *sidra* is further divided into seven portions, and each of those is preceded by a blessing. It is considered an honor to be called to the torah for their recitation. The torah is read on Shabbat, Mondays, and Thursdays during the prayer services.

Kashrut (keeping kosher)

"For I am the LORD who brought you up from the land of Egypt, to be your God; you shall be holy, for I am holy" (Lev 11:45). One of the ways in which God instructed the Jewish people to be holy is to follow the commandments of keeping kosher, also known as *kashrut*. Within *kashrut*, there are permissible foods and forbidden foods, correct ways to prepare cuisines, and prohibitions regarding the combination of certain types of food. The following section provides an overview of keeping kosher—a word that means "proper." ("Kosher" is used in other contexts besides food. For example, a *mezuzah* or torah scroll may or may not be kosher depending on whether it is damaged in some way.)

"Any animal that has divided hoofs and is cleft-footed and chews the cud—such you may eat" (Lev 11:3; cf. Deut 14:6). According to *kashrut*, permissible meat comes from ruminant animals (those that chew the cud) with cloven hooves, such as cows, sheep, and goats. Kosher poultry comes from a list of acceptable birds, as is found in the *Tanak* (chicken, turkey, geese, duck, and pigeons, for example, are permissible; owls and vultures are not). All these things have to be prepared correctly, as will be explained below.

The roots of keeping kosher are found in the Bible, which specifies that certain creatures are off-limits for the Jewish people (Lev 11:13-19; Deut 14:7-18). Scavenger birds, rodents, the camel, and the pig are listed; also, no insects are allowed. Although most Americans are not used to the idea of eating insects, it is common in other parts of the world. (The *Tanak* lists exceptions, but most Jewish authorities say it is unclear to which species of insects the rare Hebrew words refer.) What determines whether or not Jews can eat creatures from oceans, rivers, and lakes? If fish have fins and scales, they are acceptable. Examples include perch, cod, haddock, and tuna.

Forbidden sea creatures—those that lack fins and scales—include catfish, shrimp, and lobster.

Other requirements of *kashrut* include the following: animals must be checked to see that they are free of disease, blood must be drained out (the meat is salted to help accomplish this), and the sciatic nerve must be removed from the hindquarters. American kosher companies only use the forequarter of the cow because it is cost prohibitive to remove the sciatic nerve. Concerning dairy products, milk must come from kosher animals and cheese must be made with a kosher (vegetarian) enzyme.

Another important aspect of keeping kosher includes the separation of meat and dairy products, which cannot be used in the same recipe or in the same meal. This *halachah* (Jewish law) is based on the commandment, "You shall not boil a kid in its mother's milk."[20] The kosher cook knows that there are many *pareve*, or neutral products (neither meat nor dairy), that can be used in recipes that allow for versatility. In a kosher kitchen, separate utensils and dishes are used for preparing either meat meals or dairy meals.

According to *kashrut,* animals must be slaughtered humanely—as quickly and painlessly as possible. Thus, a kosher butcher (*shochet*) is trained in the proper rules of slaughtering and preparation of cuts of meat. Meat that is not properly slaughtered is called "*terefah*" (torn). *Terefah* may also refer to any food that is not kosher. Many prepared foods (such as pastries, cookies, and marshmallows) contain lard or gelatin, so if one keeps kosher, it is necessary to look for a supervisor's seal. These are provided by professionals who grant certifications and labels for prepared, packaged, and canned foods and who provide documents of compliance to Jewish law for catering companies and for kosher restaurants. In addition, professional kosher supervisors also watch over community facilities such as kosher restaurants, cafeterias, Jewish nursing homes, hospitals, schools, etc.

Regarding produce, all raw fruits and vegetables are kosher. If they are prepared, they must be made properly; for example, they must be cooked in kosher pots, be free of any insects, and cannot be formulated with any non-kosher chemicals or ingredients.

Ancient sources do not provide consistent rationales for the dietary laws. Commentators suggest a variety of possible reasons. In biblical times, the rules may have separated Israel from the pagan world, minimizing social interaction and possibilities of intermarriage. In days when other nations offered sacrifice to idols, *kashrut* would have reminded Jews not to partake in idol offerings. Also, keeping kosher is a form of moral self-discipline, for by keeping kosher, one is bound together with God and the commandments. Jacob Milgrom convincingly argues that from biblical times, Jews' restrictions on the species of creatures available for consumption show an abiding respect for life, marking reverential boundaries for God's creatures.[21] Some scholars propose that the roots of *kashrut* lie in hygienic and health-related objectives; still others emphasize the moral symbolism of avoiding wild beasts that live by violently killing other creatures and fowl who eat carrion.

In effect, in today's society, *kashrut* limits meat consumption to cows, goats, sheep, chickens, ducks, geese, and turkey; tradition underscores that these are all gentle creatures that do not live by destruction. The oral torah underscores that this discipline serves as a reminder to strive for peace. Reflecting on the spirituality of *kashrut*, Jewish commentators note that keeping kosher, in effect, forbids hunting because it requires that animals used for food be slaughtered in a quick, painless way. Judaism allows the community to use animals for sustenance, but it does not sanction hunting as a recreational sport. To be sure, there is something essentially different between eating an apple and eating a hamburger. There must be an acknowledgment that an animal's life cannot be taken for granted—for it is a creature of God.

In the land of Israel, to this day, observant Jewish farmers follow the biblical laws of tithing and of the sabbatical (the *shemitah*). Tithing requires that one-tenth of the harvest be donated to the poor. The sabbatical year necessitates that the fields lie fallow in the seventh year. Thus, if one is keeping strictly kosher, one would not eat Israeli produce in the year of the *shemitah*. The value here expressed is that the holy land belongs to God and is given to the Jewish people as tenants; God's sovereignty over the land is acknowledged in this particular way: every seventh year the land rests on its own Shabbat.

Judaism constantly strives to bring holiness into the world. It does not hold that sanctity exists only in the spiritual world and that the physical world is devoid of the divine presence. Rather, it sees infinite possibilities of bringing holiness into this material world in which people find themselves. In keeping kosher, Judaism creates a rich way to find meaning in something as fundamental as eating. In following *kashrut*, one's own table can substitute for the holiness of the temple. Sustaining life with nourishment can become a holy, spiritual act, even while being done in this physical, empirical world. The mundane and the transcendent can be inextricably linked.[22]

Denominations of Judaism in America

In America today, Jews may identify themselves as either religious or secular. Not all Jews are affiliated with synagogues, but for those who are, there are four distinct denominations: Orthodox, Conservative, Reform, and Reconstructionist congregations. It is important to note, however, that Judaism considers all Jews to be members of the same people. If one is born into a particular "denomination," for example, one does not need to convert in order to join another type of congregation or to participate in life-cycle events. The differences in the practices and beliefs stem from these congregations' unique approaches to *halacha*, or religious law. For the Orthodox, the written torah is God's revealed word, and the oral torah is composed of both God's word and the authoritative interpretation of the sages; these teachings remain in effect today. For the Conservative, *halacha* is mostly followed, but with some adjustments to modernity. In the Reform and Reconstructionist traditions, *halacha* influences tradition, but the conscience of the individual takes precedence in determining which religious practices still hold meaning in the modern world.[23]

The earliest Jewish communities in eighteenth-century America were made up of Orthodox Jews of Sephardic background who founded synagogues in Newport, Rhode Island; Savannah, Georgia; Charleston, South Carolina; Baltimore, Maryland; Philadelphia, Pennsylvania; and New York. Immigrants in the nineteenth century came from Western European—heirs of the Reform heritage, a denomination that began in Germany. These communities were followed by Ashkenazi Jews of Eastern European and Russian-Jewish ancestry who came from traditional families, settling in urban centers: New York, Philadelphia, Boston, Chicago, and Los Angeles. Today, most American Jews, a majority of whom are Reform, are of Ashkenazi ancestry. A proportionately smaller number of Jews in America are members of Orthodox, Conservative, and Reconstructionist congregations.

The Reform movement grew out of post-Enlightenment Europe in the decades after the emancipation of the Jewish communities there. During the nineteenth century, most European nations, for the first time in history, gave full citizenship to their Jewish populations. This was the first occasion when Jews had the same liberties as native citizens, including autonomy to pursue professions and to choose in which neighborhood to live. While it was true that citizenship did not mean full acceptance in the professions or within all aspects of society at large, Jews found a new normality in modern society in which their Judaism could become a religion like any other, as opposed to a defining characteristic that kept them separate from the rest of society. Reform Judaism was born in this context in the 1780s in Germany, but it was further developed in the United States, with its ideals first articulated in its Pittsburg platform of 1885. Recognizing that throughout history, Jews had adjusted to the various cultures in which they lived, the Reformers reasoned that it was an authentic Jewish expression to adapt to modern culture and practices. Their approach to *halacha* was unique, arguing that it was not of divine origin and thus was not eternally binding. Thus, *halacha*, especially in matters of dietary laws, Shabbat and holiday observance, worship services and prayer, lost its authoritative status and was to be considered under the principles of individual conscience. Reform Judaism stressed that Jews should emphasize the message of the prophets, the advancement of social justice, the improvement of society, and ethical living.

In the nineteenth and early twentieth century, Reform philosophy was heavily influenced by a hope and expectation of a universal age of the messianic times, reflecting common western European thought. Reform Judaism underscores that instead of a personal messiah and the bodily resurrection of the righteous, the community should rather hope for the messianic times and the renewal of all life. To be sure, its expectation for the perfection of humankind was destroyed after World War II and the Holocaust in which six million Jews were exterminated; nevertheless, the hope for the ideal age continues. In recent years, the pendulum has swung back, with the Reform movement once again looking to some traditional beliefs and practices for inspiration. For example, the revised Reform prayer book speaks both of the resurrection of the dead (as the Orthodox prayer book has for centuries) and the renewal of all life.[24] One of the Reform movement's most respected philosophers and leaders today, Eugene Borowitz, comments, "The subject of life after death is very difficult for moderns for many reasons, but once one understands that, there are good reasons for hoping that there is life after death. And since we know ourselves as embodied persons, the traditional terminology makes sense, although it has to be taken quite poetically."[25]

Orthodox Jews devotedly cling to torah observance and to Jewish traditions; their communities vary mostly in the degree that they are integrated into broader society. Orthodox communities can be either Hasidic or Modern Orthodox. Members of Hasidic communities, who follow the teachings of a venerable grand rabbi, or *rebbe*, receive an almost exclusively religious as opposed to a secular education. (They may, however, receive particular vocational training for professions.) The Hasidic movement began in eighteenth-century Eastern Europe, inspired by the teachings of Rabbi Yisroel ben Eliezer (1698–1760)—known as the *Baal Shem Tov* (the Master of the Good Name)—who underscored that all Jews, even the simplest person with little torah education, could serve God with joy and pious devotion. In these communities, torah learning is of the greatest value and is a lifetime and full-time pursuit for most boys and men. Girls, for the most part, receive a full-time torah education until they marry. In these tightly knit communities, it is axiomatic that the torah was divinely revealed to Moses at Sinai, that the teachings of the sages are eternally binding, and that torah principles hold primacy in all aspects of life. The way to learn torah is achieved mainly through Talmudic study and through the writings of revered *rebbes* who were the successors of the *Baal Shem Tov's* leadership. Modern Orthodox communities, in contrast, believe that torah learning can be combined with the pursuits of secular and scientific education. Members of its communities are observant but are fully integrated into secular professions.

The Conservative movement, begun in America as a reaction to the Reform movement, can be seen as a middle way between Orthodox and Reform philosophies. Much more traditional than Reform, it holds that any change from time-honored beliefs and practices must be done carefully, with the needs of the community superseding those of the individual. Conservative philosophy teaches that God revealed his will through the torah but that humans composed it throughout different periods, reflecting human perception and time-bound customs. Thus, rabbis in each generation can cautiously update the *halacha* to address new situations. The movement has ruled, for example, that it is acceptable to drive to synagogue on Shabbat, that it is permissible for men and women to pray together seated alongside one another in the synagogue, and that it is possible for women to be ordained as rabbis. In contrast, in Orthodox communities, all of these things are not accepted.

Reconstructionist Judaism, rooted in the Conservative tradition, was developed by Rabbi Mordechai Kaplan (1881–1983). It teaches that Judaism is a civilization and not a revealed faith; *halacha* consists of folkways and customs rather than the revealed will of God. Although it does not recognize that religious law is binding, it does encourage Jews to value and practice Jewish traditions, giving authority to congregations to decide which practices are meaningful and should be standard, helping its people do good in the world. As does the Reform movement, Reconstructionists hold that one can be identified as a Jew through patrilineal as well as matrilineal descent, provided that one was raised Jewish.

To be a Jew means to attach one's history and identity to the traditions and values of the people of Israel. Besides the denominations listed above, many Jews would identify themselves as "just Jewish" or as "nondenominational." For all the differences in philosophy, theology, and geography, a common narrative of the past and a shared vision of the future continue to link the people together. The Jewish people and their story endure, with many variations.

Reflecting on the practices of Judaism and on its life-cycle events, we find that as the community moves from the joyous moment of celebrating birth to the heartache of marking death, Jewish symbols, ceremony, tradition, and the commandments come together to mark life's occasions with dignity and meaning. Within the various denominations, there are differences in custom and practice, but all gathered will recognize and accept one another as members of the tribe. Rela Minz Geffen remarks that in contrast to the impersonality of the modern age, "these moments based on sentiment, family ties, and friendships enhance life immeasurably. Experiencing special moments by participating in ancient rituals in the context of a religious community . . . deepens the joy and mitigates the sadness of life and death."[26] Living a Jewish life means that every aspect of life can be infused with the teachings of torah and the wisdom of tradition and customs, no matter how these concepts are understood theologically or philosophically. Life affords daily opportunities to bring godliness into the world in both small and large ways, in thoughts, words, and action.

Notes

1. For various perspectives on the ethnic nature of Judaism, see Jacob Neusner, *Judaism in Contemporary Context: Enduring Issues and Chronic Crises* (London and Portland OR: Vallentine Mitchell, 2007) 3–50.

2. Yoel Finkelman, "A Prayer Book of One's Own," *First Things* 196 (1 October 2009): 12.

3. For a comprehensive study of Jewish prayer, see Hayim Halevy Donin, *To Pray as a Jew: A Guide to the Prayer Book and the Synagogue Service* (New York: Basic Books, 1980).

4. Marcia Falk, "Beyond Naming: Reflections on Composing the Book of Blessings," *Reconstructionist* 59/1 (1 March 1994): 67.

5. Reuven Grodner, *The Spirit of Mishnaic Law: Tractate Berachot*, vol. 2 (Jerusalem: Gefen, 1989) 483–84.

6. Nissen Mangel, ed. and trans., *Siddur Tehillat Hashem* (New York: Merkos L'Inyonei Chinuch, 1982) 46 (Deut 6:4-9).

7. Mangel, *Siddur*, 42–45.

8. Ibid., 52–60.

9. Harold Kushner, *To Life: A Celebration of Jewish Being and Thinking* (Boston: Little, Brown 1993) 232–33.

10. Quotations taken from Leo Trepp, *The Complete Book of Jewish Observance* (New York: Behrman House/Simon and Schuster, 1980) 224. For further study on the circumcision ceremony, see 219–26.

11. Maurice Lamm, *The Jewish Way in Love and Marriage* (Middle Village NY: Jonathan David Publisher, 1991) 127.

12. Trepp, *Complete Book of Jewish Observance*, 283.

13. Ibid., 286.

14. Mangel, *Siddur*, 418.

15. Ibid., 74–75.

16. Trepp, *Complete Book of Jewish Observance*, 339.

17. The translation used here is from Mangel, *Siddur*, 46–47.

18. Mangel, *Siddur*, 11.

19. Louis Jacobs, *The Book of Jewish Belief* (Springfield NJ: Behrman, 1984) 115.

20. Exod 23:19; 34:226; Deut 14:21.

21. Jacob Milgrom, *Leviticus: A Book of Ritual and Ethics*, Continental Commentary (Minneapolis: Augsburg Fortress, 2004) 106–10.

22. For further information on *kashrut*, see Herman Wouk, *This Is My God* (Boston: Little, Brown, 1988) 109–20.

23. For further information on denominations, see Ronald Isaacs, *Close Encounters: Jewish Views about God* (Northvale NJ and London: Jason Aronson, 1996) 17–22; and Leo Trepp, *Judaism: Development and Life*, 4th ed. (Belmont CA: Wadsworth, 2006) 135–51.

24. Elyse D. Frishman, ed. *Mishkan T'filah: A Reform Siddur* (New York: CCAR Press, 2007).

25. Ben Harris, "Reform Siddur Revives Resurrection Prayer," *JTA: The Global News Service of the Jewish People* (20 September 2007), http://www.ccarnet.org/media/filer_public/2011/12/09/mishkan_tfilah_jta__september_20__2007.pdf (11 June 2012).

26. Rela Mintz Geffen, "Life Cycle Rituals: Rites of Passage in American Judaism," in *The Cambridge Companion to American Judaism*, ed. Dana Evan Kaplan (Cambridge and New York: Cambridge Univ Press, 2005) 233–34.

Chapter 5

Shabbat

In the story of creation, the Bible indicates that God rested on the seventh day. The word for rest is *shavat*; from this same Hebrew root comes the word Shabbat, or Sabbath. In Jewish interpretation, it is clear that God's day of rest is the equivalent of Shabbat. On this last day of the week, Jews are commanded to rest in imitation of the Creator. It is the one day on which all creative work ceases, on which Jews purposefully reconnect with the Almighty. Since in the Jewish calendar each day begins at sundown, Shabbat commences at dusk on Friday and ends at nightfall on Saturday. What is the significance of this rest? Rest is not only for the body; it is for the soul as well. On Shabbat, the community draws nearer to God; spiritually, each individual focuses on the way in which he or she can act as a partner with God in helping to perfect creation. By resting, one imitates God because God the Creator rested on the seventh day; thus, God's sovereignty over the universe is acknowledged. In contrast to the previous days of creation, on the seventh day God fashioned nothing. Instead of creating something tangible, a distinct act was performed—the blessing of time. Time itself became holy, set apart, designated for a special purpose. As Leo Trepp says, "Because God had ceased the work of creation, the blessing and sanctification bestowed on this final day were related to no specific process or product, but to time itself."[1] This gift of time helps the Jewish people discover their link with God in holiness and their obligation to make a difference in the world. In addition, the covenant of Shabbat designated Jews as a separate people in antiquity and continues to shape their identity today: "Therefore the Israelites shall keep the sabbath, observing the sabbath throughout their generations, as a perpetual covenant. It is a sign forever between me and the people of Israel that in six days the LORD made heaven and earth, and on the seventh day he rested, and was refreshed" (Exod 31:16-17).

With these words, God instructs the Jewish people that Shabbat is an essential part of the cosmos, deliberately fashioned with specific intent and purpose. Far from being a construct of the human mind, it is as much a part of the fabric of creation as is the formation of the heavens and the earth. In keeping Shabbat, Jews imitate an essential divine activity. Observing Shabbat is commanded, a constituent part of the covenant God made with Israel. The blessings of this covenantal practice are crucial: if God was refreshed, how much more so will individuals benefit! God thus differentiates time in order to present a gift: rest is part of the providential plan of creation. It is important to note that this reference to the covenant of Shabbat is presented immediately before God gives the tablets of the torah to Moses, "written with the finger of God" (Exod 31:18). This connection of Shabbat and torah highlights the significance of a day of rest on which the very lives of individuals—both body and soul—are energized and strengthened. The torah thus teaches that God did not create the world only to abandon it. Just as God designed plants with seeds so that growth could continue in each generation, so too did God make people with a plan to sustain them in a unique and revitalizing way each week. With this renewed energy, people can tangibly live out the details of the covenant, helping to create a better world by following God's blueprint for life.

From the earliest references to Shabbat in the Bible we find that Jews included their neighbors, workers, and foreigners in the blessings of this day of rest. There are two important biblical references from Exodus and Deuteronomy:

> *Remember* the sabbath day, and keep it holy. Six days you shall labor and do all your work. But the seventh day is a sabbath to the LORD your God; you shall not do any work—you, your son or your daughter, your male or female slave, your livestock, or the alien resident in your towns. *For in six days the LORD made heaven and earth, the sea, and all that is in them, but rested the seventh day;* therefore the LORD blessed the sabbath day and consecrated it. (Exod 20:8-11)

> *Observe* the sabbath day and keep it holy, as the LORD your God commanded you. Six days you shall labor and do all your work. But the seventh day is a sabbath to the LORD your God; you shall not do any work—you, or your son or your daughter, or your male or female slave, or your ox or your donkey, or any of your livestock, or the resident alien in your towns, so that your male and female slave may rest as well as you. *Remember that you were a slave in the land of Egypt, and the LORD your God brought you out from there with a mighty hand and an outstretched arm;* therefore the LORD your God commanded you to keep the sabbath day. (Deut 5:12-15)

Both of these passages come from the Ten Commandments, as there are two versions in the Bible. Exodus gives the account of God's words to Moses at Mt. Sinai, and the words of Deuteronomy are presented as Moses' retelling to the Israelites. Because it is included in the Decalogue, the keeping of Shabbat is given a special character as one of the essential defining characteristics of the community in its relationship to God. In both passages, the effects of keeping Shabbat are far reaching, for they touch everyone in the household—all generations of families and everyone who works within the household or on the land. Even the domestic animals share in this rest—a reminder that they are God's creatures as well. And beyond the family, foreigners (the meaning of the Hebrew word "stranger" [*ger*]) are included in the practices and benefits of the broader community. In each passage, a distinct reason is given for the essential character of Shabbat. In Exodus, keeping Shabbat is likened to the rest of the Almighty; the community acts in the image of God (*imitatio dei*). In Deuteronomy, the community is reminded of the historical reality of their suffering under Pharaoh. They *know* what it is to be abused as slaves, an action that prompted God's redemption.

Jewish tradition observes another important difference in these two passages. The Exodus passage uses the verb "remember," whereas the Deuteronomy quotation employs "observe." These two verbs represent two facets of the human relationship with God. "Remember" prompts the community's members to open their hearts to God. By remembering Shabbat, one can see the harmony of creation and experience refreshment of the spirit. "Observe" appeals to the community's soul. In obeying the laws of Shabbat, Jews submit their will to the Creator, thus elevating their very being. Instead of the drive to create, achieve, accomplish, and produce that occupies life's focus during the rest of the week, Shabbat enables Jews to reconnect with God—the Source of all—in love and appreciation.

In the days of the first and second temple, Shabbat observance included two main requirements: not working and offering sacrifice. Since the time of the destruction of the second temple, prayer has replaced sacrifices as a means to draw close to God; thus, today Shabbat observance includes rest, prayer, torah study, and family and community activities. These events occur both in the home and in the synagogue. In what follows, I will outline a day of Shabbat observance from Friday afternoon to sundown on Saturday.

Friday is the preparatory day for Shabbat in which families ensure that everything needed for its observance is ready. Houses are cleaned, meals prepared, pressing business concluded. Eighteen minutes before sunset, the women of the household (in some families, the women and the girls over the age of three) light Shabbat candles, marking the beginning of the sanctification of time. With the lighting of the candles, tranquility pervades the home—in effect, the home becomes holy space with the radiance of the Shabbat light. The journalist Ari Goldman describes this transformation of the familiar into the extraordinary:

> For me, Sabbath candles still held their magic. There was a perfect moment
> of silence when [my wife] Shira would light them in our apartment . . . as
> the sun went down Friday evenings. . . . with the arrival of Shabbat, . . .
> our house would be transformed. The TV, the radio, the record player, the
> food processor and the word processor were shut off. Cooking and cleaning
> ceased. Exams and term papers were behind me. Deadlines and interviews
> were behind . . . .[2]

After the blessing recited for candle lighting, many women reserve a special time for personal prayer, expressing petition or thanksgiving. Some may recite this special prayer:

> May it be your will, Lord my God and God of my fathers, to be gracious to
> me (and to my husband and children) and to all my family, crowning our
> home with the feeling of your divine presence dwelling among us. Make
> me worthy to raise learned children and grandchildren who will dazzle the
> world with Torah and goodness and ensure that the glow of our lives will
> never be dimmed. Show us the glow of Your face and we will be saved.[3]

Many families have the custom of giving charity immediately before candle lighting by putting money in a specially designated charity (*tzedakah*) box kept at home. Parents may give their small children coins to put in the boxes, instilling the significance of considering others in this important mitzvah.

The Friday afternoon/night Shabbat service at the synagogue consists of three parts: the afternoon service (*minchah*), *kabbalat Shabbat* (the greeting of Shabbat), and the evening service (*maariv*). Essential elements include the recitation of a number of psalms, including Psalms 95–99, 29, 92, and 93—the order in which they occur in the service. These psalms underscore that it is incumbent upon people to offer praise and thanksgiving to the Creator who fashioned the world with his love and just judgments. They praise the Sovereign of the universe who structures creation according to his divine plan, in which all nations or peoples are included in his providence. Israel is reminded of its past failures in order to strive to remain loyal to the covenant; the community looks forward to a future in which the wrongs of the world will be righted and to a time when all nations will acknowledge the One God:

> Let the heavens be glad, and let the earth rejoice;
>   let the sea roar, and all that fills it;
>   let the field exult, and everything in it.
> Then shall all the trees of the forest sing for joy
>   before the LORD; for he is coming,
>   for he is coming to judge the earth.
> He will judge the world with righteousness,
>   and the peoples with his truth. (Ps 96:11-13)

An important part of the *kabbalat Shabbat* service is the recitation of the song, *Lechah Dodi* (Come, O My Beloved!). Written by Rabbi Solomon Halevi Alkabetz, a sixteenth-century scholar of torah and Jewish mysticism who taught in the holy city of Safed, the words of this song recall the message of the prophet Isaiah, who speaks of the great messianic Shabbat of redemption at the end of days. The "beloved" of the song has been interpreted to refer either to the Almighty or to the community, who gather together in welcoming this hallowed day. In the Jewish mystical tradition, God loves Israel as a bride, and Israel responds in commitment to him. Emphasizing the deepest of connections and devotion, the song is sung with great intentionality both at home and in the synagogue. The song is quite impressive in the course of the service, as the congregation turns to the entrance of the synagogue, symbolizing their enthusiastic greeting of Shabbat. Here is a selection from this song:

> Come, my Beloved, to meet the Bride; let us welcome the Shabbat . . . for it is the source of blessing . . . . Sanctuary of the King, royal city, arise, go forth from the ruins; too long have you dwelt in the vale of tears; He will show you abounding mercy . . . . Arouse yourself, for your light has come . . . . Your God will rejoice over you as a bridegroom rejoices over his bride.[4]

In this song, the community is likened to the holy city of Jerusalem that awaits redemption—a promise that is underscored with hope and joy—the sentiments that pervade the atmosphere of the service.

Following the Friday evening Shabbat service, the celebration continues in the home, in which the family shares in the best meal of the week—one marked by prayer, blessing, and song. (On occasion, Shabbat meals may also take place at the synagogue or other community center.) It is customary that the table is beautifully arranged: a white tablecloth, flowers, and china characteristically symbolize the beauty of Shabbat in a tangible way. Family and guests typically wear their best clothing. As the family gathers around the table, all join in the song, "*Shalom Aleichem*"(Peace unto You) that welcomes the ministers of Shabbat—the Shabbat angels. The Talmud relates that upon returning from the synagogue, each person is accompanied by a good angel that encourages the observance of Shabbat and a bad angel that tempts the individual to break its commandments. If a person keeps Shabbat on any given week, on the following week the good angel prevails and the bad angel submits to the good will of the family that sanctifies the seventh day, allowing the good angel to enter the home. This song welcomes those good angels: "Welcome, ministering angels, messengers of the Most High . . . come in peace, bless me with peace, pronounce a blessing over my Shabbat table." With these angels in the home, the family can put aside all squabbles or conflict, reminded of the blessings they are to each other.

This song, which sets the tone of the Shabbat meal, is followed by an excerpt from the book of Proverbs put to song, which praises Jewish women who love and encourage their family and community:

A capable wife who can find?
  She is far more precious than jewels.
The heart of her husband trusts in her,
  and he will have no lack of gain.
She does him good, and not harm,
  all the days of her life . . . .
She opens her hand to the poor,
  and reaches out her hands to the needy . . . .
She opens her mouth with wisdom,
  and the teaching of kindness is on her tongue . . . .
Her children rise up and call her happy;
  her husband too, and he praises her . . . .
Charm is deceitful, and beauty is vain,
  but a woman who fears the LORD is to be praised.
Give her a share in the fruit of her hands,
  and let her works praise her in the city gates. (Prov 31:10-31)

According to tradition, this poem is read on two levels. First, it literally praises the good deeds of the woman of the household. The model of the Jewish woman is one who acts with kindness and generosity, internalizing the torah in the actions of her everyday life. Second, the poem can be understood as an allegory that praises Shabbat (which is likened to a queen), the torah, or the divine presence.

After this tribute to women, the theme of the importance of family continues with the blessing of the children. Recalling the benediction of the priests of old, parents say to their children, "The LORD bless you and keep you; the LORD make his face to shine upon you, and be gracious to you; the LORD lift up his countenance upon you, and give you peace" (Num 6:24-27). Parents continue with blessings that link the children with their ancestors. For sons, the words first said by the patriarch Jacob to his grandsons are repeated: "God make you like Ephraim and like Manasseh" (Gen 48:20). Ephraim and Manasseh are remembered as brothers who put aside any competition for personal gain in order to serve the entirety of their people; their memory is invoked to encourage new generations to follow their lead.[5] For daughters, parents express this hope: "May God make you like Sarah, Rebekah, Rachel and Leah." These matriarchs of the Jewish people are considered models of righteousness and good deeds, remaining faithful to God even as a fledgling people who knew of great personal suffering.

With these songs and blessings completed, the ritual aspect of the meal begins. The table is adorned with a cup of wine—the *kiddush* cup (*kiddush* means "sanctification")—and with *challahs* (braided egg bread), representing the bread of the sanctuary and temple of the days of old (Num 15:17-21). Here is the prayer said over the wine or grape juice (*kiddush*):

> . . . And God finished by the Seventh Day His work which He had done, and He rested on the Seventh Day . . . And God blessed the Seventh Day and made it holy, for on it He rested from all His work . . . Blessed are You, Lord our God, King of the Universe, who creates the fruit of the vine . . . and has given us, in love and goodwill, His holy Shabbat as a heritage in remembrance of the work of Creation; the first of the holy festivals, commemorating the Exodus from Egypt. For You have chosen us and sanctified us from among all the nations, and with love and goodwill given us Your holy Shabbat as a heritage.[6]

This blessing marks the Jewish appreciation for the loving God who is both Creator and redeemer as well as the One who gives the covenant of Shabbat. Following this prayer comes the blessing over the *challah:* "Blessed are you God, King of the Universe, who brings forth bread from the earth." In biblical times, each week, the priests would eat the showbread placed on the table in the temple, of which a portion of its dough—called the *challah*—was burnt as an offering to God. Two loaves are used, signifying the two ways in which the commandment to honor Shabbat is expressed in both Exodus (*remember* the Sabbath [Exod 20:8]) and Deuteronomy (*observe* the Sabbath [Deut 5:12]); another traditional explanation is that they recall the double portion of the manna given to the Israelites in the desert on the eve of Shabbat, so that they would not gather on the day of rest (Exod 16:4-5). Thus, when approaching one's table, one does so with the same sacredness that was expressed when offering the temple sacrifices. With the blessings over wine and bread, all Jews experience the sanctity promised to Israel: "You shall be for me a priestly kingdom and a holy nation" (Exod 19:6).

Following these blessings, the meal is served. Other than the wine for *kiddush* and the *challah,* there are no required foods. In Ashkenazi homes, traditional foods include gefilte fish, chicken soup, meat, kugel (potato or noodle casseroles), and dessert. Shabbat is invariably the best meal of the week, one for which the family gathers and also guests are invited; the atmosphere is one of delight.

Following the meal, all join in the singing of the Grace After Meals (*the Birkat HaMazon*), which thanks God for Shabbat and for the provision of food, offers blessings on the family who provided the meal, and expresses hope for the future redemption. On Shabbat, the Grace After Meals is accompanied by Psalm 126, a prayer that expresses hope for the coming redemption: "May those who sow in tears reap with shouts of joy" (Ps 126:5).

As with all blessings, the words of the Grace After Meals recognize that humanity is not entitled to anything, for all is a gift from God. In discussing the various food blessings for the seven species—categories of food known from the torah[7]—the rabbis remark that whenever an individual enjoys anything of this world, "[it] requires a blessing. . . .To enjoy this world without a benediction is like robbing the Holy One, blessed be He, and the community of Israel" (Talmud, *Berakhot* 35a-b). Here are key portions of this prayer:

Blessed are You, Lord our God, King of the universe, who, in His goodness, provides sustenance for the entire world with grace, with kindness and with mercy. He gives food to all flesh, for His kindness is everlasting. . . . We offer thanks to You, Lord our God, for having given as a heritage to our ancestors a precious, good and spacious land: for having brought us out, Lord our God, from the land of Egypt and redeemed us from the house of bondage; for Your covenant which You have sealed in our flesh; for Your Torah which You have taught us; for Your statutes which You have made known to us; for the life, favor and kindness which You have graciously bestowed upon us; and for the food we eat with which You constantly nourish and sustain us every day, at all times, and at every hour.[8]

The prayers that mark the beginning and end of the meal elevate the physical act of eating into something holy—set apart from the ordinary meals of the week. The Shabbat meal joins those gathered with the Creator, linking people with both the past blessings of Israel and with hope for the future redemption—a time of peace and hope.

Shabbat Day

A unique version of the *Amidah*, the essential prayer of the daily service, is said on Shabbat day. Instead of the thirteen individual blessings that voice the community's entreaties—found in the daily service—an additional blessing underscores the holiness of Shabbat itself, accompanied by praise and thanksgiving. With this variation, the community does not call specific attention to what is missing in their lives on this one day that serves as a reminder of the goodness of creation. Even so, a general summary of God's connectedness to the spiritual and physical needs of all is recalled. Here is a capsule statement from the Shabbat *Amidah*: "Our God and God of our Fathers, please find favor in our rest, make us holy with Your commandments and grant us our portion in Your Torah; satiate us with Your goodness, gladden our souls with Your salvation, and make our heart pure to serve You in truth."[9] Shabbat strengthens the community and reminds them that in the coming week they are to serve God as partners in completing the work of creation, making God's world a better place.

The *Amidah*, in effect, serves as a substitution for the temple services. Although the idea of animal sacrifice strikes most modern people as odd at best or distasteful at worse, it is important to consider its role and importance in antiquity. Sacrifice—which included not only offerings of certain domestic animals but also of grain and wine—was understood as a way to draw near to God and to effect atonement, offered with the accompaniment of prayer. Sacrifice required that people turn their thoughts, words, and actions to God in the performance of the rites. Some sacrifices were totally burnt, but portions of others were eaten by the priests and their families and shared with the poor of the community. With this practice, the people provided for those who did not own land or who had no other means of sustenance. Maimonides understood that the practice of sacrifice made sense for the times because society felt it was the *primary* way to connect with God. Israel's sacrifices played a key role in discouraging idolatrous practices that were inimical to the ethical requirements demanded of Israel. But, ultimately, Judaism sees that the laws of sacrifice fall into the category of commandments that defy human logic; they are known only because of revelation. In carrying out these laws, the ancient community acted in accordance with God's will, showing obedience even when they could not fully understand the reason for such teachings. Even before the destruction of the temple in Jerusalem, prayer was offered not only in the synagogue but also in the home. After its destruction, prayer took on even greater significance.

With the Shabbat *Amidah*, Jews recall the temple service not out of nostalgia but in order to remember the importance of asking for God's forgiveness, doing repentance, and committing oneself to God's torah—aspects of the temple service that remain essential in any individual's relationship with God. Because Judaism teaches that the temple will be rebuilt when the messiah comes, the prayers that express hope for its rebuilding must be seen in a context of trust and expectation of the future redemption.

Torah Service

Although the torah is also read at the daily service on Mondays and Thursdays, it is on Shabbat that the greatest number of people attend services and hear the weekly torah reading. The love of torah and its importance for all Jews, no matter their station in life or their level of learning, is underscored by the ceremony that surrounds its reading. The removal of the torah from the ark in which it is housed and its replacement after the public reading are done with great ceremony and dignity. Recalling both Israel's past salvation and future redemption, the community recites these verses from Scripture: "Whenever the ark set out, Moses would say, 'Arise, O LORD, let your enemies be scattered, and your foes flee before you' (Num 10:35). For

out of Zion shall go forth instruction (torah), and the word of the LORD
from Jerusalem (Isa 2:3)." After the torah portion of the week is read, the
scroll itself (the *sefer* torah) is held up for everyone to see. The congregation
recites, "This is the torah that Moses placed before the children of Israel. It is
a tree of life for those who hold fast to it, and those who support it are fortu-
nate. Its ways are pleasant ways, and all its paths are peace (Deut 4:44; Prov
3:17-18)."[10] All are thus reminded of the importance of the precepts of
God's teachings and their link with all of Israel—both with past generations
and with those to come. As Rabbi Hayim Halevy Donin states, "In prayer,
man talks to God; through the Torah reading, God talks to man."[11]

After the torah reading of the week is completed, a corresponding portion from the Prophetic writings, called the *haftarah* ("conclusion"), is read.
The *haftarah* selections connect in theme with the torah reading. Their
recitation is preceded and concluded with special blessings said by members
of the congregation who are honored with this rite. These blessings thank
God for the prophets who spoke in the past and who continue to teach the
current generation, express hope for redemption and the coming of the messiah, give thanks for the gift of Shabbat, and anticipate the day in which all
people will know and love God. After these readings are completed, the rabbi
(or guest speaker) addresses the congregation with "a word on the torah" (the
devar torah/sermon). With the *devar* torah, the message of the weekly torah
portion comes alive. The import of the ancient text is applied to everyday
life, encouraging the people to appropriate the values of the torah lesson in
order to have an impact on everyday situations. All are encouraged to infuse
every arena of life with an awareness of God and kindness and service to
others. Following the Shabbat morning services, many congregations share a
kiddush together. The *kiddush* begins with the prayer of blessing over a cup
of wine, followed by a social gathering accompanied by refreshments or by a
full luncheon for the entire congregation. Often, individual members of a
congregation will sponsor *kiddush* in honor of a special occasion: a birthday,
wedding anniversary, or *yahrzeit* (anniversary of the death of a loved one), or
in thanksgiving for recovery from an illness.

Other activities on Shabbat afternoon might include torah study (either
at the synagogue or at people's homes), gatherings to enjoy each other's company or to hear a guest speaker, and get-togethers and games for children. At
its best, Shabbat is peaceful, meaningful, and a delight! Jews understand that
the creation of Shabbat was for the entire world. All people are given the gift
of rest. Humans are not slaves; no master, no job, no responsibilities are to

consume people, for God has designed creation for good. Jews have particular obligations on Shabbat because of their covenant with the Creator; Shabbat is a day of heightened spirituality and awareness of God's gifts, designed with the purpose of both providing for rest and strengthening people so that they can continue during the week to provide for God's creation. In a tangible way, people can see that they are not slaves to the workday world.

On Shabbat, observant Jews not only pray, gather as a community in synagogues, and enjoy meals and friendship with family and friends but also refrain from using the accoutrements of the workplace and the world of commerce. Food is prepared in advance (with some casseroles kept warm)—there is no cooking. Shopping is done ahead of time—money is not exchanged on Shabbat. Religious Jews walk to synagogues—there is no driving. Electricity is set up beforehand but is not changed on Shabbat (lights are not put on and off, computers and televisions remain off, phones are not used). For one day a week, one is not a slave to one's workplace or to the demands and pressures of the modern world. On Shabbat, religious Jews do not work. What does "not working" mean? To be sure, you do not *go* to work; if you are a farmer (the most common occupation in biblical times), you do not work in the fields. If you are an entrepreneur, you do not go to your business. Scientists and teachers do not go to the laboratory or to the classroom. How does one know what else is and is not allowed? The commandments regarding work are delineated in the oral torah. The Mishnah explains that there are thirty-nine categories of work that one cannot do. Yet any exceptions are allowed—indeed are required—to save a life (Talmud, *Yoma* 85b). These specifications are modeled on the tasks that were used to construct the holiest of places back in biblical times: the sanctuary. The sanctuary, or precursor to the temple, was the place on earth in which God dwelt in a special way, reaching out to people with love and guidance. By refraining from these categories of work, one is attuned to God's purposes of Shabbat—to prepare a better world.

In addition, there is a commandment that prohibits "transferring from the private to the public domain." In other words, one does not carry things outside of one's home. (So, for example, you would not carry a bag or push a baby stroller.) Yet the oral torah presents an ingenious solution so that one can carry things that are needed for Shabbat. Communities can build an *eruv*, or boundary, in which the enclosed area is considered their private domain. Within an *eruv*, one can transfer objects from one home or building to another. Thus, in religious Jewish neighborhoods that have an *eruv*, one can carry one's own prayer book or bring small children to the synagogue in a stroller.

In Orthodox communities, Jews gather once more toward the end of Shabbat to offer the afternoon and evening service. The conclusion is followed by *havdalah* ("separation"), a brief ceremony that distinguishes the holiest of days from the ordinary weekdays. *Havdalah* can be said at home or in the synagogue. It includes a blessing over wine, symbolizing the bounty of God's goodness; a blessing over sweet-smelling spices, representing people's ability to enjoy the good things of creation; and a blessing over the light from a braided candle, signifying that God is the source of all wisdom and enlightenment. Thanking God for making both the holy and the ordinary things in the world, *havdalah* also looks forward to the future perfection of the creation. By hearing the blessings, seeing the flame, tasting the wine, and smelling the spices, one uses all the senses in recognizing that this very world is infused with holiness and that the sanctity of Shabbat can enter the ordinary days of the week. This prayer ends with everyone wishing each other, "Have a Good Week!" and with the song *"Eliyahu ha Navi"* (Elijah the Prophet) that encapsulates the hope for the coming of the messiah and the transformation of the world for good: "May Elijah soon come to us, with the messiah son of David."

All of the commandments of Shabbat—those that tell the community what to do in the service of God and those that proscribe certain activities— construct an unparalleled moment of holiness in time. We conclude with the reflections of the revered American Jewish philosopher Abraham Joshua Heschel:

> Six days a week the spirit is alone, disregarded, forsaken, forgotten. Working under strain, beset with worries, enmeshed in anxieties, man has no mind for ethereal beauty. But the spirit is waiting for man to join it. . . . What is the Sabbath? Spirit in the form of time. With our bodies we belong to space; our spirit, our souls, soar to eternity, aspire to the holy. The Sabbath is an ascent to the summit. It gives us the opportunity to sanctify time, to raise the good to the level of the holy, to behold the holy by abstaining from profanity.[12]

Notes

1. Leo Trepp, *The Complete Book of Jewish Observance* (New York: Behrman House/Simon and Schuster, 1980) 66.

2. Ari Goldman, *The Search for God at Harvard* (New York: Ballentine, 1991) 99–100.

3. Lori Palatnik, *Friday Night and Beyond: The Shabbat Experience Step-by-Step.* (Northvale NJ: Jason Aronson, 1994) 6–7.

4. Nissen Mangel, ed. and trans., *Siddur Tehillat Hashem* (New York: Merkos L'Inyonei Chinuch, 1982) 131–32.

5. Palatnik, *Friday Night and Beyond,* 20.

6. Mangel, *Siddur,* 146–47.

7. Based on Deut 8:8, the seven species are wheat, barley, grapes, figs, pomegranates, olives, and dates. In Hebrew, "honey" refers both to the nectar made from the honeycomb and to the preserves made from dates.

8. Mangel, *Siddur,* 89–90.

9. Ibid., 180.

10. The translations of the biblical quotations in this paragraph are quoted from Mangel, *Siddur,* 187.

11. Hayim Halevy Donin, *To Pray as a Jew: A Guide to the Prayer Book and the Synagogue Service* (New York: Basic Books, 1980) 234.

12. Abraham Joshua Heschel, *The Sabbath: Its Meaning for Modern Man* (New York: Farrar, Straus and Giroux/First Noonday Press, 1975) 65–75.

Chapter 6

Holidays

Just as Shabbat is an essential component of the sacred that marks each week, so too do the religious holidays bring an awareness of holy time throughout the calendar year. These sanctified times link Jews both to the Almighty and to each other as they recall essential aspects of God's connection with his people that spans the boundaries of time. The holidays not only recollect how God dealt with Jewish forebears in the past and how he revealed the torah but also how he continues to be in relationship with Jews today on the deepest and most intimate level, permeating all aspects of life.[1]

Rosh Hashanah

Rosh Hashanah, which means "The New Year," is not at all like the American New Year's Day. It is a solemn yet joyful religious holiday—a day of judgment for the entire world. This quotation from the Mishnah captures the theme of divine examination: "On Rosh Hashanah all human beings pass before him as troops, as it is said, 'the Lord looks down from heaven, He sees all mankind. From his dwelling place He gazes on all the inhabitants of the earth, He who fashions the hearts of them all, who discerns all their doings (Ps 33:13-15)'" (Mishnah, *Rosh Hashanah* 1.2).

On Rosh Hashanah, the community also celebrates the birthday of the world, acknowledging God as king and calling out to him in prayer and supplication. Judaism teaches that God hears people's pleas for mercy, especially when accompanied by good deeds, charity, and repentance. People pray that their names will be "inscribed in the Book of Life" for the coming year.

The Rosh Hashanah services, which span two days (in September or October), include torah readings about the birth of Isaac and the struggles of Hagar and Ishmael (Gen 21), the binding of Isaac (Gen 22), the birth of Samuel (1 Sam 1:1–2:10), and God's promise to restore the exiles to the land of Israel (Jer 31:1-19). These readings underscore the compassion of God for all humanity, as the name "Hagar"—the foreigner—implies. Although Hagar and Ishmael were expelled from Abraham's household, God heard their cries and offered life and blessing. The birth of Isaac to a long-barren couple shows that God is true to his promises and that people have cause to hope even in the darkest of hours. Paradoxically, God summoned Abraham to offer his son as a sacrifice to him. Abraham was obedient to the point of stretching forth his knife-wielding hand; nonetheless, God rescinded the command, seeing that Abraham's devotion was resolutely unconditional—a sign to the world that Abraham was worthy of God's covenant. The birth of Samuel the prophet to the barren Hannah shows not only God's compassion for the suffering of the individual but also his care for Israel in the revelation of his word throughout the prophet's mission. Still, Judaism acknowledges the reality that the world continues in brokenness and that the Jewish people remain in exile. The words of the prophet Jeremiah promise a different future:

> Hear the word of the LORD, O nations,
>   and declare it in the coastlands far away;
> say, "He who scattered Israel will gather him,
>   and will keep him as a shepherd a flock." (Jer 31:10)

The themes of the holiday are both somber and hopeful. This consciousness is brought to mind: human beings fail in their responsibilities to God and to one another. But this is not a cause for despair; God shows his side of compassion in a unique way during the season of Rosh Hashanah. There are infinite opportunities for repentance and commitment to good deeds, for the God of Mercy not only fulfilled his oath to Abraham and Sarah but also promises a new future to all of Israel—one in which the suffering of exile will cease and the world will be perfected according to his will. In this context, the struggle for personal growth in one's relationship with God is ongoing, marked by limitless potential for attachment.

One of the most anticipated moments of the Rosh Hashanah service is the sounding of the shofar—the ram's horn—a simple musical instrument on which one can make three sounds: one sustained note and two broken tones. These simple, plaintive echoes cry out to both the community and to God. These sounds without words represent the people's most heartfelt yearnings that cannot be articulated and evoke the image of a weeping, penitent heart. The call of the shofar resounds to the community: "Sleepers, arise from your slumber. . . . Review your actions, repent your sins, and remember your Creator! . . . Look into your souls and improve your ways and your deeds. Let all abandon the ways of evil and thoughts that offer no benefit."[2] In addition, the sounding of the shofar stirs the response of God's compassion, as it were, for he recalls the binding of Isaac. In the interpretive tradition of Genesis 22, God's test of Abraham—commanding him to sacrifice his son—and the patriarch's astounding obedience provide a storehouse of merit for subsequent generations. Even though the sins of the community may feel staggering, the actions of the righteous—of whom Abraham is paramount—serve not only to inspire the current generation but also appeal to God's mercy even today.

The customs of Rosh Hashanah proclaim the hope and joy of this holiday. At the Rosh Hashanah meal, symbolic foods are used. Apples dipped in honey indicate expectations for a sweet New Year ahead. The pomegranate, with its abundant seeds, signifies the people's appeal for God's many blessings. Round loaves of challah adorn the Rosh Hashanah dinner table, symbolizing the crown of God the King—the Creator who sustains the world and who judges its inhabitants with mercy. On Rosh Hashanah, it is customary to pray for forgiveness at a body of water so that sins can be symbolically "cast away," expressing the belief that God will hear the plea of the repentant heart, as captured in this prayer:

Who is a God like you, pardoning iniquity
and passing over the transgression
of the remnant of your possession?
He does not retain his anger forever,
because he delights in showing clemency.
He will again have compassion upon us;
he will tread our iniquities under foot.
You will cast all our sins
into the depths of the sea. (Mic 7:18-19)

Within Jewish tradition one finds the image of the heavenly books in which the deeds of the individual are recorded and in which one is sealed for life or death in the coming year. Thus, Jews greet each other during the New Year season with the words, "May you be inscribed and sealed in the Book of Life!"

Yom Kippur

Yom Kippur means "The Day of Atonement." On this day of fasting and prayer, which occurs nine days after the beginning of Rosh Hashanah, people strive to make amends and repair the wrong they have done throughout the year, hoping to become reconciled with people and with God. Judaism teaches that God pardons and that people are capable of change. Each year, the community is called to turn back to their essence—accomplished by repentance, charity, and doing good deeds. People are capable of binding their souls with the will of the Almighty. Thus, it is customary for parents to give the following blessing to their children on Yom Kippur that underscores the tradition of living a life of faithfulness to the torah:

> May it be the will of our Father in Heaven to place into your heart love and fear of Him. May the fear of God be upon you always so that you never sin. May your yearnings be for Torah and *mitzvos* [commandments and good deeds]. May your eyes see straight ahead, may your mouth speak wisdom, and may your heart feel awe. May your hands engage in *mitzvos*, your feet run to fulfill the will of your Father in Heaven. May He grant you sons and daughters who are righteous, who will be engaged in Torah and *mitzvos* throughout their lives. May your livelihood be blessed and may your sustenance be earned in a permitted manner, with ease and bounty from His generous hand, rather than from the gifts of flesh and blood; sustenance that will leave you free for the service of God. May you be inscribed and sealed for a good and long life among all the righteous of Israel.[3]

Yom Kippur is not only a time to consider the sins that one has done on occasion throughout the past year but also a time of introspection in which the individual considers what habits of life and characteristics of personality led one to living less than a righteous life. The stakes are high, for life without God would feel empty—an existence close to death! Indeed, the characteristics that mark daily life are suspended on Yom Kippur. The laws established by the Bible and by the sages in antiquity are still followed today. There is no eating and drinking, no bathing, no anointing with oil, no marital relations, and no wearing of leather shoes (considered the most luxurious footwear). In Jewish practice, fasting means no food or drink from sunset when Yom Kippur begins to the nightfall of the following day. To be sure, children and those who are sick do not fast; in fact, if fasting would endanger one's health, it is forbidden. Children start to fast when they reach *bar/bat mitzvah* age—which is thirteen years old for boys and twelve years old for girls. On this day, Jews come as close as possible to considering—in the most tangible of ways—what it would be like to be without the love of God and the life-giving precepts of the torah.

Yom Kippur is considered a "Shabbat of Shabbats"—a day of complete rest and devotion to God in which meditation on ways to change one's life for good is paramount. Forgiveness rests not only on the relationship between humanity and God but also on the connections individuals have with their fellow human beings. Thus, people must ask forgiveness of one another before Yom Kippur begins. During the days between Rosh Hashanah and Yom Kippur, Jews ask forgiveness of one another for the hurtful things they have done against their family, friends, and neighbors during the previous year. On Yom Kippur itself, the entire congregation publicly acknowledges their faults in prayer and asks God for pardon for the sins committed against him.

During Yom Kippur, the services stress the importance of prayer, repentance, and charity as ways to recommit to God. Key components of the Yom Kippur services include *Kol Nidrei* ("All Vows"), the Confession, the Recounting of the Acts of the Martyrs, and readings from the torah and the book of Jonah. The stirring melody of the *Kol Nidrei* prayer asks for forgiveness for all unfulfilled vows, promises, and for sins of speech. Historically, it is rooted in the period of the Spanish Inquisition (late fifteenth-early sixteenth century), when Jews were forced to take vows that disowned their faith. During the morning service, the righteous acts of the martyrs of the past are recited; the accounts of their sacrifices remind the community of the extraordinary acts of their ancestors and prompt a heartfelt call upon God's mercy. The Scripture readings detail the ceremonies of atonement in the days of the temple (Lev 16:1-34; Num 29:7-11), a time when the high priest would perform rituals that purified God's dwelling place with sacrificial offerings and would cleanse the community of their sins by dispatching a goat (a "scapegoat") to the wilderness; the animal would symbolically carry away the iniquities of the people. Despite the strangeness of the ancient idea that sin was viewed as something tangible—and was contagious if not physically removed—the spiritual idea of the scapegoat ritual remains extraordinary: that God so cared for the community that he provided a concrete means for the people to communicate with him, plead for atonement, and draw near despite their failings. As it was then, so, too, it is today: individuals strive to appeal to God, renewing their relationship with the energy that comes from forgiveness. The torah reading is followed by the *haftarah* from the book of Isaiah (57:14–58:14) that underscores the necessity of connecting good deeds with a meaningful fast: "Is this not the fast that I choose: to loose the bonds of injustice, to undo the thongs of the yoke, to let the oppressed go free, and to break every yoke?" (Isa 58:6). During the afternoon service, the book of Jonah is read, in which the congregation is reminded that, as did this prophet, one sometimes enters into repentance reluctantly. But if God forgives even the subjugators of Israel—the people of Nineveh (Assyria) and their animals(!)—so too can a striving, sincere community expect God's love and compassion. Reminded of Jonah, who hesitates to believe his own words that announce God's compassion, the community is called on to remember this proclamation: "you are a gracious God and merciful, slow to anger, and abounding in steadfast love, and ready to relent from punishing" (Jonah 4:2).

One of the prayers that is recited many times over the course of the services of Yom Kippur is the Confession (*Viduy*). In this prayer, each individual is willing to share in the responsibility of the community, as the prayer is addressed in the collectivity. The list of sins points out the ubiquity of human failures yet the steadfastness of a forgiving King. In the Hebrew language in which this prayer is recited, the list of sins forms an acrostic—they are given as an alphabetized list—saying, in effect, that the totality of sinful acts is akin to "an alphabet of woe," thus heightening the community's remorse.

> Our God and God of our fathers, may our prayer come before You. . . . We have sinned. We are guilt laden, we have been faithless, we have robbed, we have committed iniquity, caused unrighteousness, have been presumptuous, have counseled evil, scoffed, revolted, blasphemed. . . . You search the innermost recesses, testing men's feelings and heart. Nothing is concealed from You or hidden from Your eyes. May it therefore be Your will to forgive us our sins, to pardon us for our iniquities, to grant remission for our transgressions. . . . Behold I am before You like a vessel filled with shame and confusion. May it be Your will . . . that I may no more sin, and forgive the sins I have already committed in Your abundant compassion.[4]

With this confession, the community says, in effect, "We have committed sins from A to Z. We know that You are judge of all. We beg for your forgiveness and mercy." Although any one individual may not have committed a particular transgression, the communal aspect (*we* have sinned) shows the connectedness and responsibility of Jews with and for one another. Indeed there is the saying, "All of Israel is responsible for one another" (Talmud, *Shavuot* 39a).

Although Yom Kippur is the most solemn day of the year, it is not sad. A deep sense of peace comes from the act of atonement; repentance enables an individual to feel reconciled with God. All the feelings of estrangement and failure can be cast away, knowing that, in sincerity, one has a chance to stand before God in renewed harmony, in closeness, with energy and hope. Repentance has the power to transform the way an individual interprets his or her failures. Instead of seeing one's shortcomings or unkindness as impediments to one's relationship with God or with others, one can look at past failings and hurts as a way to effect change for good. Alienation and shame can be transformed into powerful springboards for love, for caring, and for friendship when it is seen that one can emulate the same compassion that God shows to humans. Judaism thus sees repentance as transformative. In becoming close to God on Yom Kippur, one can become more devoted to those in one's life. When Yom Kippur is over, the acts of apologizing, confessing sins out loud, giving charity, and resolving to live a kinder, generous, more loving life culminate in a renewed commitment for the coming year.

Sukkot

> Now, the fifteenth day of the seventh month, when you have gathered in the produce of the land, you shall keep the festival of the LORD, lasting seven days; a complete rest on the first day, and a complete rest on the eighth day. On the first day you shall take the fruit of majestic trees, branches of palm trees, boughs of leafy trees, and willows of the brook; and you shall rejoice before the LORD your God for seven days. . . . You shall live in booths for seven days; all that are citizens in Israel shall live in booths, so that your generations may know that I made the people of Israel live in booths when I brought them out of the land of Egypt: I am the LORD your God. (Lev 23:39-43)

According to the torah, the Israelites were protected by God's sheltering presence when they were led out of Egypt. Having departed in haste and pursued by Pharaoh's troops, the Israelites were delivered at the Red Sea, but they lived in terrible uncertainty in the wilderness. In this context, the people made temporary shelters in the desert—small huts or booths that were a far cry from permanent, substantial dwellings. While moving from Egypt to the promised land, the liberated slaves voiced complaints to Moses, even stating that they missed the security of Egypt! Rather than abandon them, God responded with reassurance and love, providing manna to eat and shelter that would comfort their fears, giving them a refuge from their contingent existence. In this context, the people learned to trust God even as they lived the difficult lives of wanderers. In the absence of security they found that only God could bring true refuge. There was only one thing they could rely on—God's protection.

Today, during the festival of Sukkot (which occurs in September or October), Jews remember God's sheltering presence and relive it in their own communities in a concrete way. In the yards of individual homes and apartment buildings, as well as in institutions (Jewish schools, community centers, synagogues), people build simple, temporary huts of wood or canvas, with roofs made of a natural material (tree branches, bamboo, corn husks), to symbolically experience God's presence as in the days of the wilderness wanderings. With these *sukkahs* (booths), Jews remember that despite deprivation or impoverishment, riches or success, all depend on God. Sukkot is a time in which to rely on God alone, symbolized by these humble structures in which one dwells. In these unassuming shelters, people pray, share a meal, and visit with one another. On Sukkot, one is reminded that God's protection occurred not only in a distant and foreign land, but it still exists today in countless ways in peoples' lives. Eating, praying, and gathering in the *sukkah* shows the community that God cares for all people: young, old; rich, poor; simple, complicated. This paradigm reminds people that all need to be open to one another as well.

Sukkot is a holiday of guests—both invited friends and the spiritual guests of Jewish tradition. The torah teaches that seven guests come to visit the *sukkah*—one for each night. Abraham, Isaac, Jacob, Moses, Aaron, Joseph, and David are all remembered as ancestors who experienced exile—Abraham and Jacob in Paddan-aram, Isaac in the kingdom of Abimelech, Joseph in Pharaoh's Egypt, Moses and Aaron in the wilderness, and David in the Judean desert. These ancestors are remembered for their faithfulness to God in times of great uncertainty, when they were wanderers without homes. Their righteousness and kindness are understood to have merit and blessing. In the spirit of hospitality, people invite friends and acquaintances into the *sukkah* to enjoy a meal and to share their blessings and friendship.

In the days of the temple, the community took on a special responsibility of praying for the world on the holiday of Sukkot, offering sacrifices for each nation. Thus, this holiday emphasizes that all humankind must turn to its Creator in thanksgiving for their blessings and in repentance for wrongdoing, as they strive to be partners with God in making the world a better place.

A unique aspect of Sukkot is use of the *lulav* and *etrog* for prayer, in obedience to the commandment to offer blessings on various plants during this holiday. The *lulav* is a bouquet consisting of three plants: the willow, myrtle and palm; the *etrog* is the fruit of the citron plant. Together, the *lulav* and *etrog* are lifted up in prayer and procession during the synagogue services and throughout the week of Sukkot, serving to bless the holiday. Each element of the bouquet has a separate symbolic meaning, representing four paths to the Almighty. The totality of these approaches shows that God needs all people to be part of his plan—no matter their strength or shortfalls in striving to serve the divine purpose. Tradition holds that the *etrog*—which has both a lovely flavor and fragrance—symbolizes Jews who are knowledgeable in torah and who practice good deeds; the palm tree—which has taste but no scent—refers to those who are versed in torah learning but lack acts of kindness. The myrtle—which has fragrance but no taste—represents those who have good deeds but whose torah knowledge is wanting, and the willow— which has neither taste nor aroma—refers to those who lack both wisdom and the practice of the commandments.[5] Yet all complement each other and are encompassed in God's protecting guidance. God includes all in his sheltering love, and the community is in need of all its members.

Shemini Atzeret and Simchat Torah

At the end of the weeklong celebration of Sukkot, the community celebrates the "Eighth Day of Assembly" or Shemini Atzeret. In Israel this holiday is combined with Simchat Torah, the festival of the "rejoicing in the torah"; in the diaspora (lands outside of Israel), the two holidays are held on sequential days. The Eighth Day of Assembly is marked by a holy day of rest in which the prayer for rain is offered for the first time of the upcoming winter season (in Israel, the rainy season typically starts in late October and continues through late April). It is the last day on which one spends time in the *sukkah*—a time to cherish this last day of closeness with the divine presence. On Simchat Torah, the community completes the reading of the last portion of Deuteronomy—the end of the Five Books of Moses—and begins the new liturgical cycle with the reading of Genesis. The congregation marks the joy of the holiday by singing and dancing with the torah scrolls, in procession around the *bimah*—the altar on which the holy text is read. By completing the torah and beginning anew at the same service, the community shows its dedication, celebrating the fact that God has accepted the repentance of the community that began on Rosh Hashanah.

Hanukkah

In the midst of the darkness of winter (November–December) comes Hanukkah, the Festival of Lights. Hanukkah marks the miracle of oil that occurred in the days of the oppressive Syrian-Greek rule in the land of Israel (second century BCE) when Judah the Maccabee led a revolt against the tyranny of Israel's overlords. Victorious, he went to purify the temple that had been desecrated with foreign idols and offensive alien sacrifices. Judah the Maccabee was successful over the Syrian-Greek king, Antiochus Epiphanes (reigned 175–164 BCE), oppressor of the Jewish people. During his reign, the hegemony of Greek culture at first threatened Jewish life because of its appeal to Jews, some of whom, on their own, abandoned ancestral practices in order to be more acceptable to the broader population. Eventually, under Antiochus, what began by the choice of some continued by force against all Jews: the practice of Judaism was outlawed, and the continuation of the Jewish people itself was threatened. Circumcision and Shabbat observance was proscribed, and the temple was polluted with sacrifices to foreign gods. During the worst days of this despotic rule, a small band of Jews led by Judah the Maccabee revolted against the king. Amazingly, they were victorious against the imperial army. They marked their victory by purifying the desecrated temple. Although there was only enough pure oil to burn for one day, a miracle allowed for an eight-day supply of oil, so that the light could shine while new oil was being prepared. Thus, Hanukkah is observed for eight days.

As Jews have celebrated the holiday over the centuries, emphasis has been placed on the ways in which God has protected the Jewish people throughout their history during the times they have fought persecution and assimilation. During Hanukkah, Jews light an eight-branch menorah (plus one additional light for the server or kindling candle)—one candle on the first day, increasing with one additional candle on each successive day. Candles are lit every evening in a window of the home, symbolizing that the light of faith is to be spread out into the world. The celebration is accompanied by eating traditional foods: potato pancakes and jelly doughnuts—foods fried in oil—reminiscent of the miracle of oil in the temple. Children play dreidel—clay tops that are spun for small cash prizes—recalling those times when Jews had to conceal any participation in religious practices. The story is told that during the days of Antiochus's persecution, Jews had to designate a lookout to announce if soldiers were advancing to investigate whether Jews were studying torah. If an official were to approach, those assembled would take out dreidels, pretending that the game of chance was the reason for their gathering. The four faces of the dreidel each have a letter that stand for the words of this sentence: "A great miracle happened there." (In Israel today, the dreidels read, "A great miracle happened *here*"!)

During Hanukkah, the following prayer is said that captures the essence of the holiday:

> And [we thank You] for the miracles, for the redemption, for the mighty deeds, for the saving acts, and for the wonders which You have wrought for our ancestors in those days, at this time . . . when the wicked Hellenic government rose up against Your people Israel to make them forget Your Torah and violate the decrees of Your will. But You, in Your abounding mercies, stood by them in the time of their distress. . . . You delivered the mighty into the hands of the weak, the many into the hands of the few, the impure into the hands of the pure, the wicked into the hands of the righteous, and the wanton sinners into the hands of those who occupy themselves with Your Torah. . . . Then Your children entered the shrine of Your House, cleansed Your Temple, purified Your Sanctuary, kindled lights in Your holy courtyards, and instituted these eight days of Chanukah to give thanks and praise to Your great Name.[6]

With the celebration of Hanukkah, Jews remember the acts of defiance from those who refused to surrender their faith for alien ways. Each person is reminded that he or she contains within himself or herself a light of God's presence that can penetrate the darkness of the world.

Tu B'Shevat (the Fifteenth of the Month of Shevat)

During biblical times, farmers were obligated to tithe the produce of their trees according to a specified seven-year cycle. Because the trees have been nourished by the preceding winter rains, any fruit produced after the fifteenth of the Hebrew month of Shevat (corresponding to January–February)—the time when, in Israel, the trees first show new signs of life—was considered to belong to the New Year. In effect, Tu B'Shevat is a "New Year for Trees." It is an occasion to acknowledge that the gifts of the land of Israel come from God's design. Because this holiday celebrates nature, it has also become common for people to participate in the charitable activities of the Jewish National Fund, a worldwide organization that supports forest restoration and water reclamation in Israel. Some people donate money, others individually plant trees in Israel in memory of or to honor a loved one.

In more recent years, some Jews have revitalized the ancient custom of having a Tu B'Shevat *seder* (a special ritual meal). The Tu B'Shevat *seder* of Hillel (a Jewish outreach program for college-age Jewish students), for example, emphasizes some of the important ecological teachings of Jewish tradition. It cites this telling passage from the Midrash:

> When God created Adam, God took him around all the trees of the Garden of Eden and said to him: "see how wonderful and praiseworthy all of my creations are. Everything I have created, I created for you. Be careful not to destroy My world; for if you destroy it, there is no one who will fix it after you." (Midrash, *Ecclesiastes Rabbah* 7:19)[7]

Present-day celebration of Tu B'Shevat is marked by a consciousness of God's gifts of life-sustaining fruit and of his care for the land of Israel, as well as the gift of the wellspring of torah. Based on a unique interpretation of Deuteronomy 20:19, in which the text asks, "Is man a fruit of the tree?" a spiritual comparison is made between people and trees. Just as God nurtures the roots of the tree, God sustains a person with faith. The tree stands tall, reaching out to the heavens, itself the posterity of the seeds that came before it. So, too, an analogy is made with the Jewish people, who are encouraged to emulate the kindness and love of their ancestors, ever being renewed and growing spiritually. The tree is adorned with leaves, parallel to the importance of torah; and the most precious product of the tree, its fruit, is likened to the outcomes made from a person's good deeds.

On Tu B'Shevat, it is customary to eat from the special produce mentioned in the Bible that are associated with the bounty of the land of Israel: olives, dates, grapes, figs, and pomegranates (Deut 8:8). When eating one of these fruits for the first time of the year, Jews recite the blessing that marks special occasions: "Blessed are You, O Lord our God, king of the Universe, who has sustained us and enabled us to reach this season." This prayer is followed by the unique blessing for fruit: "Blessed are You, O Lord our God, king of the Universe, who bring forth the fruit of the tree." Marked by these prayers and the act of tasting a new fruit of the season, tradition holds that both trees and humans follow a cycle of renewal, rooted in the acts of the Master of the Universe.[8]

Purim

How is God's providence manifested in the world? Jewish history teaches that the Almighty's ways can be dramatic or miraculous, such as occurred during the exodus, or subtle, as happened in the days of post-exilic Persian-Jewish community who lived during the days of King Ahasuerus. Although the extermination of the Jewish community was planned in chilling detail, the courage of one Jewish woman led to the salvation of the entire community. On the holiday of Purim, Jews read the story of this deliverance that is found in the biblical book of Esther. The story recounts the days when the Persian sovereign unwittingly married a Jewish subject, who was advised by her guardian to keep her identity secret in uncertain times.[9] While she was queen, the king's chief minister, Haman, exposed his genocidal intrigue:

> There is a certain people scattered and separated among the peoples in all the provinces of your kingdom; their laws are different from those of every other people, and they do not keep the king's laws, so that it is not appropriate for the king to tolerate them. If it pleases the king, let a decree be issued for their destruction, and I will pay ten thousand talents of silver into the hands of those who have charge of the king's business, so that they may put it into the king's treasuries. (Esth 3:8-9)

Ahasuerus's evil, though more subtle than that of Haman, was equally dangerous, for in his silent acquiescence he allowed Haman to take active steps to implement his murderous plan. Armed with superstition, Haman cast lots for the most propitious day on which to attack the Jewish people. The lots were known as "*pur*"—plural *purim*—hence the name of the holiday.

A crucial part of the Purim story is the effect of the terror that, at first, paralyzed the queen who feared for her life to speak up before the capricious king. But Mordecai, her guardian, encouraged her: "Who knows? Perhaps you have come to royal dignity for just such a time as this" (Esth 4:14). With these simple yet profound words of reassurance, Esther acts, setting in motion a series of events in which the Persian-Jewish community is allowed to defend itself. They are victorious over their attackers. Yet no intervening angel, no miracles, precipitate their triumph. Indeed, no direct reference to God is found in the book of Esther. But a profound truth can be discerned: the hidden hand of God lies behind the scenes. Esther's courage led to a surprising, improbable feat that never could have been imagined. Miraculous things transpired because Esther resolved not to keep silent.

The book of Esther is beautifully written by hand on a parchment scroll, called the *megillah*, and is read aloud with the entire congregation's involvement, as the listeners are invited to drown out the name of the villain—Haman—who designed the genocide of all Jews in his realm. The congregants use fanciful groggers (noisemakers) to obliterate the sound of the foe's name as it comes up in the text. With the completion of the *megillah*, the people say a blessing, concluding with these words: "Praised are You, Lord our God, who saves His people Israel from all their enemies, for You are a redeeming God."

Despite the seriousness of the theme of the book of Esther, the presentation of the story is marked by humor and irony. King Ahasuerus marries Esther because he deposes his first wife, Vashti, the queen who threatened his own authority to such an extent that it imperiled the kingdom. All men feared that their wives might give orders to their husbands! Yet Ahasuerus ends up listening to his second wife, a Jewish woman. The villains of the book threatened to murder innocent people but were instead vanquished in battle or suffered capital punishment by the order of their own king (Esth 7:9; 9:14). Thus, the tone of the holiday is one of levity and gladness, despite what ultimately could have been catastrophic. As Arthur Waskow says, the story uses "hilarity and humor to cure the soul of fear and to shatter the pompous pretensions of all tyranny."[10] Indeed, the genocidal enemy of the Jewish people is remembered as a cookie! It is a Purim tradition to eat triangle-shaped treats known as *hamantashen*—"Haman's pockets."[11]

This delightful holiday (which occurs in February–March) is also marked by communal celebratory meals, parades, the wearing of costumes, and the performance of plays and skits, all based on the idea of God's presence in concealment. In addition, people give charity to the poor and provide charming gift baskets of food for friends, in imitation of the acts of Esther's community who made "days of feasting and gladness, days for sending gifts of food to one another and presents to the poor" (Esth 9:22). Everyday life, in large ways and small, can hold within it the hidden ways of God. Purim shows that at any moment, any individual's action can not only change the course of his or her own life but also contains infinite possibilities to touch the lives of others.

Pesach (Passover)

"We were slaves of Pharaoh in Egypt," and the Lord our God brought us forth from there "with a strong hand and an outstretched arm." If the Holy One, blessed be He had not brought forth our ancestors from Egypt, then we and our children, and our children's children, would still be enslaved to Pharaoh in Egypt. Therefore . . . it is our duty to retell the story of the Exodus from Egypt. (The Hagaddah)[12]

Passover celebrates the redemption of the Jewish people from Egypt. As the book of Exodus relates, the Israelites were enslaved until God, who designated Moses as his spokesman, rescued them from Pharaoh. In Jewish tradition, Passover not only celebrates the redemption of the Jews of long ago but also that of every Jew alive today, for this holiday of freedom marks God's liberation from anything that prevents a person from being bound together with him. This belief is rooted in the first Passover because the liberation from Egypt provided freedom from slavery with a particular purpose: Jews were freed in order to receive the torah and in order to become servants of God.

On the first two nights of the eight-day holiday (which is observed in March–April), families and friends gather at home for the Passover *seder*: a ritual meal in which the Haggadah, the story of the exodus and its interpretive tradition, is told, ritual foods are eaten, and a festive meal is enjoyed. The symbolic foods encapsulate the essence of the commemoration. A spring vegetable (such as celery or parsley), dipped in salt water, as well as bitter herbs (horseradish) represent the tears of suffering and bitterness of slavery; a chopped apple mixture represents the mortar that held together the bricks that the slaves were forced to make; a roasted egg and a shank bone recall the Passover sacrifice from antiquity. Everyone eats *matzah*, the unleavened bread that sustained the Jews as they escaped from Egypt in haste—without time for their bread to rise. At the *seder*, the *matzah* is raised up, with those around the table proclaiming: "This is the bread of affliction which our ancestors ate in the land of Egypt. All who are hungry—let them come and eat. All who are needy—let them come and celebrate the Passover with us. Now we are here; next year may we be in the land of Israel. Now we are slaves; next year may we be free" (The Haggadah).[13]

During the reading of the Passover Haggadah, everyone recites this key text:

> In every generation one must see oneself as though having personally come forth from Egypt, as it is written: "And you shall tell your child on that day, 'This is done because of what the Lord did for me when I came forth from Egypt.'" It was not our ancestors alone whom the Holy One, blessed be He, redeemed; He redeemed us too, with them, as it is written: "He brought us out from there that He might lead us to, and give us, the land which He had promised to our ancestors." (The Haggadah)[14]

Judaism teaches that in every generation, each person should feel as though he or she personally were redeemed from Egypt. Thus, the Passover is not something that happened only once in history; it has eternal significance for the Jewish people—it must be retold and relived.

In the days and weeks before Passover begins, people clean their homes of all traces of leaven. Throughout the eight days of this holiday, Jews refrain from eating any food with leaven, as it is understood to symbolically represent human arrogance before God. Indeed, Passover is a time to reflect on the ways in which each person can rid himself or herself of any negative parts of the human spirit that keep one in a state of alienation from the Almighty. Not only governments but also one's own personal life, with its sorrows, fears, and habits, can enslave or distance one from the divine presence. One can hope for radical change in one's life: once a slave does not mean always a slave. Furthermore, people can work alongside God as partners to redeem the world. Recalling the past experience of slavery reminds the community to empathize with people who are suffering. The Passover celebration emphasizes that the memory of the origins of a despised, powerless people can be transformed into a compassionate attitude toward others.

Counting of the Omer and Lag B'Omer

As we read in Leviticus, the second day of Passover was marked by a special offering of a measure of grain in the sanctuary (Lev 23:15). From the evening of this sacrifice until the arrival of the holiday of Shavuot (the Festival of Weeks), people counted the seven weeks of the intermediate time. This "counting of the omer" (the omer is a unit of measure), which is still observed today, links these two major festivals: Passover—the holiday of redemption—and Shavuot—the holiday that marks God's bequest of the Ten Commandments. At the time of the exodus, the intermediate period was marked by the wilderness wanderings. Its culmination at Shavuot makes evident the purpose of the liberation and the trials in the desert: the giving of the commandments and Israel's renewal of its commitment to be servants of God. With the counting of the omer, the community remembers that their liberation from slavery and their obligations to follow the torah are inextricably linked.

Because of the solemnity of this period, Jews refrain from participating in weddings and observe certain mourning practices (for example, not going to concerts, shaving, or getting haircuts). But on one day of the period of the omer, known as Lag B'Omer (the thirty-third day of the period of counting), the mourning practices cease. This is a happy holiday of weddings, picnics, parades, and bonfires.

Two important Jewish sages are associated with this holiday, although the origins of these connections are unclear. According to one tradition, the disciples of Rabbi Akiva were delivered from a plague on Lag B'Omer. Another custom honors the memory of Rabbi Shimon bar Yochai, the author of the mystical text, the Zohar. In Israel, many religious Jews make a pilgrimage to his gravesite in the city of Meron.[15]

Shavuot (Weeks)

Forty-nine days after Passover comes the festival of Shavuot—the Feast of Weeks. In ancient times, this was one of the pilgrimage festivals in which people from throughout the countryside would travel to Jerusalem to offer their sacrifices of the firstfruits of their harvests (Lev 23:17). The counting of the omer culminated with a special offering of two loaves of bread in the temple.[16] After the destruction of the temple, another aspect of the holiday was emphasized: the giving of the torah to the Jewish people on Mt. Sinai. The Israelites were freed from the slavery of Pharaoh (commemorated with the Passover) in order to become servants of God. Thus, the instructions of the covenant—the blueprint for living according to God's ways—were revealed at Sinai where the Israelites arrived after seven weeks of wandering in the wilderness. As the Bible relates, God's unique revelation gave the people the stipulations of the covenant. This torah, consisting of the Ten Commandments, other written commandments, and their oral interpretation and significance, were given to the entirety of the community gathered at the mountain. There, the people agreed to be God's servants, saying, "Everything that the LORD has spoken we will do" (Exod 19:8). In Jewish tradition, it is understood that all souls were present—even those of people not yet born (Deut 29:10-15 [9-14 Heb]). Jewish teaching underscores that the torah was given to all members of the Jewish community. Israel—that is, the entirety of Israel—is called "a priestly kingdom and a holy nation" (Exod 19:6). Ordinary people—and not only priests—experience everyday acts that are called to be sanctified. Thus, the totality of the tradition can be traced back to this life-altering day that occurred once in time. Because the torah has quintessentially defined the Jewish people, this holiday serves to recall its importance in a tangible celebration. On Shavuot, the community, in its worship service, again agrees to accept the torah.

The book of Ruth is connected to Shavuot not only because it recalls the days of the harvest festival but also because it tells the story of a Moabite woman who entered into the community of Israel, three generations before King David. Her faithfulness to her newly adopted community is praised. This unlikely woman, an impoverished foreigner, became the great-grandmother of King David. Jews are reminded that converts—both past and present—are indeed vital members of the community. Their acceptance of the torah makes them complete members of the Jewish people.

Customs of the holiday of Shavuot include decorating homes and synagogues with plants and flowers, reminiscent of harvest time and suggestive of nature's bounty. In addition, people eat dairy foods, remembering God's promise "to deliver them from the Egyptians, and to bring them up out of that land to a good and broad land, a land flowing with milk and honey" (Exod 3:8). On Shavuot, both the Ten Commandments and the book of Ruth are read in the synagogue. It is considered a commandment to hear the reading; thus, synagogues are crowded with all members—even babies and small children—for this portion of the service. The Midrash recounts that when God offered the Decalogue, he asked for a guarantor from the men and women gathered at Sinai. The only suitable pledge was their children, whom God accepted. This Midrash points to the importance of teaching torah to subsequent generations, forming an indissoluble link among the generations. The awe-inspiring reality of the revelation is reflected in this Midrash on the Ten Commandments: "When God gave the Torah no bird twittered, no fowl flew, no ox lowed, none of the angels stirred a wing, the seraphim did not say 'Holy, Holy,' the sea did not roar, the creatures spoke not, the whole world was hushed into breathless silence and the voice went forth: 'I am God, your God'" (Midrash, *Exodus Rabbah* 29:9).

Tisha B'Av (The Ninth of Av)

Tisha B'Av (the ninth of [the Hebrew month of] Av, corresponding to July–August), a day marked by fasting, prayer, and the reading of the book of Lamentations, commemorates the destruction of the two temples in Jerusalem. The first temple was destroyed by the Babylonians in 587 BCE, and the second by the Romans in 70 CE. Both acts were associated with the death and exile of thousands of Jews—to the lands of the Babylonian and Roman empires, respectively. The Hebrew month of Av is also a time in which other tragedies occurred, including the expulsion of the Jewish communities from England (1290) and from Spain (1492), and catastrophes of

the twentieth century—the outbreak of World War I (1914) and the depor-
tations to the Warsaw Ghetto (1942) during World War II.

Jews refrain from hosting weddings and celebrations during the three-
week period that precedes this holiday, beginning with the Fast of the 17th
of the month of Tammuz (the preceding Hebrew month)—the date when
the beginnings of the Babylonian siege of Jerusalem began. On Tisha B'Av
itself, Jews fast, read from the books of Lamentations and Job, and read from
other Talmudic texts concerning mourning. Additional teachings include
refraining from washing, anointing, and the wearing of leather shoes.

In biblical times, the temple represented the manifestation of God's presence in the world, showing that the arenas of the divine and the material
could be linked. Showing that God created the world so that he would have
a place in which to dwell, it served as a meeting ground of heaven and earth
and as a center of torah learning. With its absence, the heart of the Jewish
people is wounded. Owing to the wisdom of Rabbi Yochanan ben Zakkai
(c. 30–90 CE), who—risking his own life—begged the Romans to spare the
city of Yavneh during their suppression of the Jewish revolt against imperial
rule, Jewish learning survived even without the presence of the temple in
Jerusalem. Yavneh became the new seat of torah learning. Nevertheless,
Jewish tradition still includes prayers for the building of the third temple in
the days of the messiah—a time in which the final redemption will occur,
when all the world will see the fullness of God's plan for his creation, and
when God's presence in the world no longer will be concealed.

Reflecting on the totality of the holidays that fill Jewish life throughout
the year, Rabbi Harold Kushner concludes,

> Every fall, the Jewish calendar offers us days of solemn majesty, days of
> cleansing and reconciliation, days of remembering to be grateful for the
> good things of the earth and world. Every winter, Hanukkah summons us
> to light candles to chase the darkness. Every spring, Pesach comes with its
> Seder meals, with its food, wine, family memories, and message of libera-
> tion. . . . the Jewish calendar calls on us to stop defining ourselves by what
> we do for a living or what we fill our days with, and asks us to define our-
> selves by who we are and who we might be.[17]

Indeed, in celebrating the holidays, the spirituality and holiness of the world
are linked with memory and physical acts. The community's senses are filled
with palpable symbols, unique foods, and distinct commandments. Hearts
and minds turn to God and to each other with moving prayers, melodies,

and the sounding of the shofar. The holidays constitute a precious legacy that every generation passes on to the next, helping to keep the spirit of the Jewish people, their connection to God, and their identity with each other alive.

Notes

1. Michael Strassfeld, *The Jewish Holidays: A Guide and Commentary* (New York: Harper and Row, 1985); Leo Trepp, *Judaism: Development and Life*, 4th ed. (Belmont CA: Wadsworth, 2006) 350–77; and Arthur Waskow, *Seasons of Our Joy: A Handbook of Jewish Festivals* (New York: Summit Books, 1982).

2. Rambam, *Hilchos Teshuvah* 3, quoted in Eliyahu Kitov, *The Book of Our Heritage: The Jewish Year and Its Days of Significance*, vol. 1 of Tishrei-Shevat, adapted and expanded ed., trans. Nachman Bulman (Jerusalem and New York: Feldheim, 1997) 17.

3. Kitov, *Book of Our Heritage*, 71.

4. Jacob Neusner, *A Short History of Judaism: Three Meals, Three Epochs* (Minneapolis: Augsburg Fortress, 1992) 117–18.

5. *Leviticus Rabbah* 30:12.

6. Nissen Mangel, ed. and trans., *Siddur Tehillat Hashem* (New York: Merkos L'Inyonei Chinuch, 1982) 90.

7. "Trees, Creation and Creativity: The Hillel Tu B'Shevat Seder," Hillel's Joseph Meyerhoff Center for Jewish Learning, http://www.hillel.org/NR/rdonlyres/A5339C76-6B07-4EC1-A970-D8FAFBA5E1CC/0/tu_bshevat_seder.pdf (13 June 2012).

8. See "The New Year of Trees: Why We Celebrate the New Year of Trees," from the talks of the Lubavitcher Rebbe, Rabbi Menachem M. Schneerson, http://www.chabad.org/library/article_cdo/aid/149854/jewish/The-New-Year-of-Trees.htm (13 June 2012).

9. For discussion on the historicity and genre of Esther, see Michael V. Fox, *Character and Ideology in the Book of Esther*, 2nd ed. (Grand Rapids MI: Eerdmans, 2001) 131–52.

10. Waskow, *Seasons of Our Joy*, 116.

11. In Israel, the cookies are known as *oznei Haman*—Haman's ears.

12. *Passover Haggadah*, new rev. ed., ed. Nathan Goldberg (Hoboken NJ: Ktav, 1993) 9.

13. Ibid., 8.

14. Ibid., 23–24.

15. Strassfeld, *Jewish Holidays*, 47–54.

16. Ibid., *Jewish Holidays*, 70.

17. Harold Kushner, *To Life!: A Celebration of Jewish Being and Thinking* (Boston, Toronto, and London: Little Brown, 1993) 142.

Israel

Extending back to the biblical era, the narrative of Judaism clings to a persistent future hope: the time of the messiah will be marked by an ingathering of the exiles to Zion, the land of Israel. In this time of the final redemption, the city of Jerusalem fulfills its divine mission: to instruct the world in the ways of God's peace (Isa 2:3). Throughout centuries of diaspora living, Jews have kept this ideal alive in their prayers, traditions, and ceremonies. As descendants of the patriarchs and matriarchs who lived in the ancient land, slaves who left Egypt to bring the covenant into the holy land, and kings who built Jerusalem as a city that would proclaim the one God to the world, Jews hold that they are irrevocably tied to the history of the land of Israel. Although the modern state of Israel came about because of historical and political—and not ostensibly religious—forces, the connection of this long-stateless people to their country formed a key impetus among the founders of the modern Zionist movement. This late nineteenth- and early twentieth-century quest for a Jewish homeland culminated in the founding of the modern state of Israel in 1948. Jews' feelings about the contemporary state of Israel can be heard in the words of an American Rabbi, Ammiel Hirsch, who wrote of his ascent to Mt. Nebo in Jordan—repeating Moses' journey. Unlike Moses, who never entered the promised land, this contemporary rabbi had the chance to enter Israel's borders. He reflected,

> Standing atop that mountain in the presence of eighty rabbis, spiritual leaders and descendants of a people who should have died one hundred times over, I felt the wind of God blow across my face. After all these centuries, after all the tragedies, we were still here, looking at the Promised Land from the very spot where Moses breathed his last. And we were about to enter the sovereign Jewish state! The centuries had not dimmed our vision; our vigor was unabated.[1]

This love for Israel has a long history.[2] When Jews enter the land of Israel—and especially the city of Jerusalem—it is as though they have arrived home. Jews have professed that the land of Israel is part of the covenantal promise, a gift from God that was never abrogated. Although not part of any official teaching, the role of divine providence in paving the way for the birth of the modern state cascades in the lyrics and poetry of Jewish texts, prayers, and songs. The continued existence of the people despite centuries of attempted eradication is itself considered a miracle. The words of the national anthem of Israel, *HaTikvah* (the Hope), reflect this belief:

> As long as the Jewish spirit is yearning deep in the heart,
> With eyes turned toward the East, looking toward Zion,
> Then our hope—the two-thousand-year-old hope—will not be lost:
> To be a free people in our land,
> The land of Zion and Jerusalem.

The Bible refers to Zion and Jerusalem on more than 600 occasions. Everyday prayer, the grace after meals, and daily psalms refer to the holy city multiple times. The Passover *seder* concludes with the words, "Next year in Jerusalem." But even within the city, participants say these words that look to the future because Jerusalem both exists in time and yet lies beyond it. Jerusalem is both the real city and the ideal place that will exist in the messianic age.

The rise of nationalism in the nineteenth century, the emancipation of Jews in Europe, and the long European history of anti-Semitism and violence led to the rise of Zionism in the late nineteenth and early twentieth centuries.[3] Zionism is the political philosophy that holds that Jews should be allowed to have a homeland, just like any other people. Jews—with the exception of small populations in the Kinneret (the Galilee)—were expelled from the land of Israel since the Roman period (and had no independent sovereignty in the land since the Hellenistic period), but they never gave up their hope and dream of returning to their land. With the rise of nation states in the eighteenth and nineteenth centuries, Jews, too, began the search for a homeland, hoping to live freely under their own autonomous government, at liberty to pursue either a secular or religious life. Although, on occasion, other lands were suggested as a country for the Jewish people, from the beginning of the movement Jews predominately spoke about the return to Zion—the biblical homeland.

European journalists, politicians, and intellectuals gathered at the first
Zionist Congress in Basel, Switzerland, in 1897. Organized by Theodore
Herzl (1860–1904), it outlined its goals for settling Jews in Palestine. During
this period, the land of Israel, known as Palestine (a name given by the
Romans), was a part of the Ottoman Empire, ruled by Turkish officials. In
1917, with the promulgation of the Balfour Declaration, the British Empire
declared its support for the formation of a Jewish homeland in Palestine.
After World War I, in which Britain and the Allies defeated the Ottoman
Empire, Palestine was placed under British rule. From this land was carved
Jordan, established as a semi-autonomous kingdom, and Palestine, governed
by the British Mandate (under the League of Nations). Yet, because of Arab
opposition to Jewish settlement, Britain increasingly pulled back on its support. It placed limits on immigration, extending even into the World War II
era, when thousands of Jews who were fleeing Europe were turned back at
Palestine's coast. Despite its illegality under British rule, Jews were smuggled
into Palestine during the period of the war by Jewish residents who operated
clandestinely.

In the aftermath of the war, it became clear that the world turned its
back on the Jewish people. For the few Jews who had the opportunity to
escape Nazi lands, there was no place for them to go. After the Holocaust
(the *Shoah*), the vow "never again" took on a new urgency. In 1947 the
United Nations directed that Palestine should be divided into two states—
one for Jews and one for Palestinian Arabs—with complicated borders
drawn according to the identity of local populations.[4] Although Jews
accepted the plan, Arabs rejected it, vowing to drive Jews into the sea. Under
the leadership of David Ben Gurion (1886–1973)—who would become the
first prime minister of Israel—Jews declared their independence on May 14,
1948. The next day, when the British left the country, war broke out
between Jews and Arabs. Despite the participation of armies from surrounding Arab lands (Lebanon, Syria, Jordan, and Egypt), Israel won an unlikely
victory. Arabs who remained in Israel during the war were given Israeli citizenship, but those who fled into Syria and Egypt were never given local
citizenship, and Israel did not allow the majority of refugees to return to the
land in its newly created borders. Only Jordan offered citizenship to (most)
refugees; all others were stateless. With its victory and new borders, Israel was
in control of west Jerusalem, but Jordan controlled the eastern section of the
city. East Jerusalem included the Jewish quarter of the Old City, the Mount
of Olives cemetery, and the Western Wall (the remnant of the temple); yet all

of these places of the eastern sector were off limits to Jews—Jerusalem became a divided city.

The Arab rejection of the right of Israel to exist led to another war in 1967.[5] In 1967, Egypt, Syria, and Jordan prepared to attack Israel from the Gaza Strip, the Golan Heights, and the West Bank (of the Jordan River)—lands then under Arab control (by Egypt, Syria, and Jordan, respectively). Immediately after the Arabs demanded an end to the United Nations' patrol of sensitive border regions and prepared to invade, Israel attacked.[6] The Arab coalition lost the 1967 war, with Israel occupying these lands (Gaza, the Golan Heights, and the West Bank—including East Jerusalem) that had an Arab majority. Two approaches were given to these territories. On the one hand, certain regions were annexed in order that Jerusalem no longer be a divided city and in order to have defensible borders. This victory was incalculable for psychological, religious, and strategic reasons, for under Jordanian rule no access was given to Jews for either the Western Wall (the only remnant of the ancient temple compound) or for the Jewish quarter of the Old City. Nonetheless, acts of terror, both in Israel and throughout the world, increased and culminated in the 1973 war (the Yom Kippur war), in which the Arabs declared war on Israel. Despite heavy casualties, Israel won; an armistice agreement ended the fighting on January 18, 1974.

A weighty problem today in Israel concerns the lands captured in 1967 and defended in 1973. In 1979, Israel returned the Sinai to Egypt. That truce remains in effect today, but it is now tenuous because of the instability of the Egyptian government that has existed since the 2011 deposing of President Hosni Mubarak. Since the Oslo Accords of 1993, Israel's majority position has been that, with the exceptions of a united Jerusalem and defensible borders—the specifics of which are debated—the nation would be open to exchanging lands of the West Bank and Gaza for peace. Still, the Israeli position is that to return to the exact borders of 1967 would be indefensible and that giving the right of return to all Palestinian refugees and their descendants would eliminate the Jewish state. According to the Oslo Accords, the Palestinian Authority was to set up an independent government, and settlement of the refugee problem and disputed lands was to begin in 1996.[7] About 95 percent of the lands in the West Bank and the Gaza Strip would be returned to Palestinian rule, with the other 5 percent to be negotiated. (The most intractable problem is the status of Jerusalem, which Palestinians want as their capital. In addition, in various West Bank lands, Israeli settlers have built homes and towns, the status of which is controversial.) Yet, since this agreement, the outlines of the plan have broken down. The peace process has been stalled ever since, complicated by the fact that in 2010, Palestinian rule was divided into two factions. The West Bank is the seat of the ruling party Fatah and the home of the Palestinian authority's president, Mahmoud Abbas, whereas Gaza is under the rule of the opposition party Hamas, which includes in its charter that the state of Israel has no right to exist and that the entirety of Israel be given to Palestine. A breakthrough in this decades-long stalemate will require compromises of historic proportion.

Today, when critics argue that Israel should be a secular state for both Jews and Arabs, Jews see—in light of their history—an intolerable picture. No nation in either Europe or Arab lands ever accepted Jews as equals, and no ruling nation of the land of Israel ever granted them freedom. Entitled to a country, no more or less than any other nation, Jews tenaciously guard the right for Israel to exist, even as the world hounds it for its imperfections. The "never again" of the Holocaust still resounds in memory, as do terrorist bombings and desecration of Jewish holy sites. For even today, there are nations who hold that the Holocaust never existed and that Israel should be swept into the sea. There are Jews from throughout the world and Israelis who are supportive of the idea of a two-state solution, but to imagine an Israel again with a divided Jerusalem and with indefensible borders or daily terrorist bus bombings is untenable. Great compromises are required.

From its inception in 1948, the state of Israel is not only the country of Israelis but is also, in a sense, the country of all Jews from throughout the world. According to the Israeli constitution, the "Law of Return" specifies that Jews from any country have the right to immigrate to Israel as citizens (to make *aliyah*). From its founding, Israel has taken upon itself the responsibility of protecting Jews from wherever they have been endangered. When the state was created in 1948, the Jewish population of Israel was 600,000. Today this tiny country of 10,000 square miles holds 5 million Jews and 2 million non-Jews. In the late 1940s and 1950, displaced persons—survivors of the Holocaust—came to Israel when no other country welcomed them. After the state was declared and surrounding Arab nations reacted to their Jewish communities with reprisals, entire Jewish communities from Iran, Iraq, Yemen, Libya, Morocco, Tunisia, and Egypt immigrated. Since the dissolving of the Soviet Union, more than a million Jews have come from former Soviet bloc countries. In the late 1980s and the 1990s, more than 20,000 endangered and destitute members of the Ethiopian Jewish community were clandestinely airlifted to Israel. Every continent is represented, as Jews from North and South America, South Africa, and Australia have come in hopes of living a dream of being in a Jewish democracy where they could live freely in a Jewish cultural and religious context, to whatever degree they wish to participate. Today, half the world's population of Jews lives in Israel. Any governmental action has world Jewry in mind, as these words of Ammiel Hirsch indicate:

> Whatever Israel does, it does in the name of the Jewish people. . . . Its values are Jewish values. Its accomplishments are Jewish accomplishments. Its flaws are Jewish flaws. This is how most Jews see it. This is how most of the world sees it. . . . The [Jewish] people requires the attributes of people-hood—land, language, culture, religion, sovereignty, self-determination, to expand Jewish identity and cultivate the deep roots of Judaism.[8]

Israel is the only place in the world where Jews are guaranteed self-determination and a life free from anti-Semitism. Although Israel is infused with Jewish values and culture, it was not established as a theocracy according to torah law; rather, it is a democracy. Indeed, in the worldwide secular age in which humanity finds itself today, Israeli life reflects this reality. Jews in Israel (as they are worldwide) may be torah-observant or not. But they share a common peoplehood and culture, however diverse. In Israel currently, more people identify themselves as "secular" than "religious." Yet the demarcation between secular and religious, as it applies to Judaism, is misleading. Secular Jews in Israel have a strong Jewish identity as a member of the nation and people. They may not recite daily prayers or attend weekly services, but they strongly identify as Jews, know the history and customs of Judaism, and participate in life-cycle events (marriage, *bris, bar* and *bat mitzvahs*, weddings, burials) and holidays.

Attacks on Israel's very right to exist continue even today. Iran threatens to use nuclear weapons. Many Europeans hold Israel to an impossibly high standard, blaming every Middle Eastern problem on the singular non-Arab state. In America today, an increasing number of people argue that because Israel is a Jewish state, it is by definition racist. Others argue that the nation is too militaristic. Most Jews today would agree that there is nothing wrong with critiquing any particular policy of the modern state of Israel. But to use political criticism as a springboard to question the very existence of the country is considered offensive. No other nation state is held to that kind of scrutiny. As Jews see it today, it is often the case that the world holds Israel to a higher standard of perfection that it does other nations.[9]

In previous chapters of this book, we have seen the importance of religious holidays in forming and reflecting the character of the Jewish people. It is appropriate to study four additional memorials—all instituted in Israel within the twentieth century—that help to illustrate the character of the state. They are Holocaust Remembrance Day (Yom HaShoah), Memorial Day (Yom HaZikaron), Independence Day (Yom HaAtzmaut), and Jerusalem Day (Yom Yerushalayim).

In 1953, the state of Israel established Yom HaShoah, Holocaust Memorial day. *Shoah* means "catastrophe" in Hebrew; it is the word used in Israel and in much of Europe to refer to the Holocaust—the Nazis' systematic extermination program to annihilate all of Europe's Jewish population. With their reign of terror, killing squads, and death camps, the Nazis destroyed two-thirds of the European Jewish community, some 6 million people. Yom HaShoah has been marked with talks and reminiscences from survivors (although as the years pass, there are less and less of these elderly people), commemorative programs, documentaries, and music, as well as accounts of Jewish resistance and survival. Remembrances include study of the unique culture of the Jewish communities of this vanished world. The underlying message is the importance of remembering, so that the horror of this unfathomable genocide will never be repeated. At Yad Vashem, the Holocaust museum and memorial in Jerusalem, a state ceremony is held in which the prime minister, president, chief rabbis, and survivors participate, saying prayers and paying tribute. Such ceremonies are repeated throughout the country, and it is a day on which theaters and public entertainment venues are closed out of respect for the solemn occasion.

The civic holiday Yom HaZikaron was also instituted by the state; it commemorates both the fallen soldiers and the victims of terrorist attacks. After the United Nations decided to partition the British Mandate of Palestine in 1947, Israel's future president, Chaim Weitzman, was attributed with saying, "The state will not be given to the Jewish people on a silver platter." The Israeli poet Natan Alterman (1910–1970) depicts the sacrifices made by Israelis for the formation of the nation and for the continued security of the state surrounded by hostile neighbors. His poem, "Silver Platter," is often read on Israel Memorial Day. In this poem, the country looks to two young soldiers:

... Full of endless fatigue
And all drained of emotion
Yet the dew of their youth
Is still seen on their head

Thus like statues they stand
Stiff and still with no motion
And no sign that will show
If they live or are dead

Then a nation in tears
And amazed at this matter
Will ask: who are you?
And the two will then say

With soft voice: We—
Are the silver platter
On which the Jews' state
Was presented today

Then they fall back in darkness
As the dazed nation looks
And the rest can be found
In the history books.[10]

This poignant poem underlines the sacrifices made by Israeli soldiers during their nation's wars. There is a deep appreciation in the country that the very existence of the state comes only with constant vigilance and sacrifice. The entire day is marked by admiration and esteem for the fallen. All public entertainment ceases; broadcasts from radio and TV all mark the bravery of those who perished. Sirens are sounded twice during the day, at which point everyone stops what they are doing (even traffic comes to a standstill), and people pause to remember the dead. Ceremonies include the reading of the names of those who died and the recitation of the *kaddish* (the memorial prayer for the dead).

The solemnity of Yom HaZikaron is soon followed with the festive celebration of Yom HaAtzmaut, Israeli Independence Day. Occurring in mid-May, this joyous state-sponsored holiday is marked by parades and public celebrations that honor Israeli achievements in all spheres of life. On this day, the prestigious Israel Prize is given to citizens who have contributed to science and culture. There are public celebrations with singing, folk danc-ing, and other performances.

Observed in late spring (on the twenty-eighth day of the Hebrew month of *Iyar*), Yom Yerushalayim (Jerusalem Day) celebrates the reunification of the city that took place after the 1967 war. (As explained above, from 1948 to 1967, while east Jerusalem was under the control of Jordan, Jews were for-bidden all access to the Old City and the Western Wall.) The day is marked not only by outdoor concerts, parades, and celebrations but also with a reli-gious component, as psalms of praise are said in most synagogues.

For Jews throughout the world today, the attachment to Israel encom-passes a variety of feelings: emotional, political, theological, historical. The connection can be compared to a love relationship. When the appeal goes out to send money to support the rescue of Jews who need to be brought to Israel, the community inevitably finds enough resources. Jews feel a connec-tion that pushes them to care deeply for one another. This watchfulness is evident in the upstart nation that blossomed from limited resources, absorb-ing millions of immigrants while all along fighting for its very existence. It is the tangible expression that the people of Israel can exist in peace and secu-rity, with their lives self-determined—and not at the mercy of another government. Jews throughout the world know they can be good citizens of their own countries, but they can also support, take pride in, and love the state of Israel, sustaining it both as a refuge for Jews fleeing political persecu-tion, anti-Semitism, or economic devastation and as a nation in which Jews can simply live according to their own culture and faith.

My family's dear friend, Harold Frolkis (of blessed memory), was com-mended for having served in the Israeli army, protecting the security of the Jewish people in Israel. At his eulogy, his close friend, Samuel Abady, remarked of this American-Jewish immigrant,

In the post-Holocaust world, some Jewish writers and philosophers embraced the image of the Jew as essentially wounded, a man racked by his Jewishness. For this kind of Jew, the world is a desert, and God is shrouded in silence. The theme of life is exile, the challenge of life is living with a kind of brave despair. Harold rejected this worldview. He was a man who overcame his past, both personal and tribal. He was a true Zionist in heart and soul, a genuinely liberated Jew. He often called me and talked in Hebrew just for the joy of it. For him, being a Jew was not living life as a wounded man, but instead, the acme of spiritual health. The world was not a desert, but an orchard of possibilities in which Jews could rejoice in

their freedom, strengthened by their commitment that "all Israel is one."
To know Harold was to know that the principle of *ahavat Yisrael* [love of
the Jewish people] animated every fiber of his being. Harold took deserved
pride in his accomplishments in building a thriving business from scratch,
and providing for his family. But deep down, the thing which gave him the
greatest pride of all was that he served. He never referred to the army as
simply *Tsahal* [the Hebrew acronym for "The Defensive Army for Israel"]
or the Israel Defense Force. Instead, he would say: "I'm a soldier in the
Army of the Jewish People."[11]

I find that Frolkis's life, as reflected in these words, is truly representative of
the connectedness that Jews throughout the world feel for each other:
responsibility, pride, and an unbreakable bond.

Judaism is ultimately a faith of great optimism, and its people hold fast
to an ideal that the world can become a better place and can be perfected
under God's design. From the revelation of God to Abraham, Jews learned
that monotheism demanded an ethical counterpart. With Moses, Jews
understood that societies could be enhanced by the torah and the establish-
ment of a judicial system. Humanity can become partners with God to
improve the world. A tangible sign of that vision is the hope of Zion in
which Jews can leave the tragic aspects of their history behind and embrace
their vision of future restoration and peace. Israel has provided a haven from
pogroms, persecution, and anti-Semitism; it ensures Jewish survival and provides hope. It is a place that nourishes Jewish culture and values while
embracing Jewish history and the connectedness of the people with one
another.

Notes

1. Ammiel Hirsch and Yaakov Yosef Reinman, *One People, Two Worlds: A Reform Rabbi and an Orthodox Rabbi Explore the Issues That Divide Them* (New York: Schocken, 2002) 36.

2. Leo Trepp, *Judaism: Development and Life*, 4th ed. (Belmont CA: Wadsworth, 2006) 157–76.

3. Ian Bickerton and Carla Klausner, *A History of the Arab-Israeli Conflict*, 5th ed. (Upper Saddle River NJ: Pearson, Prentice-Hall, 2007),15–64; Charles D. Smith, *Palestine and the Arab-Israeli Conflict: A History with Documents*, 6th ed. (Boston and New York: Bedford, St. Martin's, 2006) 23–58.

4. Bickerton and Klausner, *History of the Arab-Israeli Conflict*, 65–111; Smith, *Palestine and the Arab-Israeli Conflict*, 170–214.

5. Bickerton and Klausner, *History of the Arab-Israeli Conflict*, 133–54; Smith, *Palestine and the Arab-Israeli Conflict*, 264–305.

6. Trepp, *Judaism*, 165.

7. Smith, *Palestine and the Arab-Israeli Conflict*, 450–65.

8. Hirsch and Reinman, *One People, Two Worlds*, 226–68.

9. Harold Kushner, *The Case for Israel—Yom Kippur 5771*, http://www.tiofnatick.info/index.php?option=com_content&view=article&id=266:the-case-for-israel&catid=63:rabbi-harold-kushner-sermons&Itemid=194 (accessed 12 June 2012).

10. Natan Alterman, "The Silver Platter," translated from the Hebrew by David P. Stern from the website, "Taking a Personal Stand on Israel: A Yom Ha-Atzma'ut Resource from ARZA," http://www.arza.org/_kd/Items/actions.cfm?action=Show&item_id=2074&destination=ShowItem (accessed 12 June 2012).

11. Samuel A. Abady, "Eulogy for Harold G. Frolkis (Nov 8, 1955–Oct 16, 2007)," given on 18 October 2007 at The Jewish Community Funeral Home, Milwaukee WI.

Conclusion

In Judaism, God, Torah, and Israel are the three pillars that undergird prospects for a meaningful life of faith, provide a context to live ethically and morally, and open a warm and welcoming community that marks time with joy and celebration. These mainstays become foundational to map one's life experiences of reality, to construct significance and purpose, and to connect with God. Despite the presence of a world permeated with suffering, Judaism believes that God created it as an ordered, meaningful place. The shattered condition of the world calls out for humanity to work as partners with the Almighty to infuse the world with godliness. Defying the philosophies or theologies of modernity that hold that existence precedes essence or that suffering is beyond the purview of God, Judaism boldly declares that everything has a purpose—even those things humanity cannot possibly fathom. It proclaims that God guides and judges the world with justice and mercy and includes in its teachings infinite narratives of Jews who nullified their own will for a greater good.[1] With such ideals and models, Jews are given guideposts to navigate experiences and choices in everyday life, all the while connected with an extended family and vibrant culture. The Jewish conception of God allows its people to see the everyday acts of waking, seeing, eating, and loving as expressions of blessing. It allows one to hope that God, who has a plan that lies beyond human capacity for discernment, can use even the brokenness of the world. It gives its people a worldview that declares life can be sanctified.

How does one know about this God? Judaism accepts that not all reality is empirically verifiable. Revelation exists—the quintessential event being the revelation at Sinai that occurred upon the redemption from Egypt. This first redemption not only becomes paradigmatic for the history of the Jewish experience but also touches each individual personally. In every generation there are tyrants, crushers of human freedom, threats to existence itself. Yet Judaism's narrative asserts that God has structured a universe so that, ultimately, evil will not prevail. And even in times of prosperity and freedom, myriad experiences can keep an individual from God—loss, suffering, sadness, angst. Jewish teaching insists that this person, too, can be brought out of a personal state of slavery.

Judaism does not keep these paradigms of hope and meaning in the abstract. Rather, Sinai is about leaving slavery behind and then following a specific path that continues even now. How deeply one becomes immersed in the tradition is a matter of both choice and devotion. The offerings of the various Jewish communities from throughout the world reflect this commitment to lifetime torah learning and engagement with each other. From the nursery school to the yeshiva, from synagogue classes to informal lessons held in peoples' homes, from individual instruction by the rabbis to out-of-town retreats, from fundraising to volunteer activities, there are countless choices to give structure to the Jewish journey. With the teachings and commandments given at Sinai, former slaves entered an unfamiliar land with the new purpose to have every aspect of life infused with ethics and righteousness—in short, infused with holiness. To be holy means to be set aside, designated for a special purpose. Every aspect of life—eating and drinking, relationships with family and institutions, business, agriculture, government, education, treatment of the poor and the stranger—were governed by the teachings at Sinai. Because all were from Moses, and ultimately from God, nothing could be subsumed; nothing could be placed outside the realm of torah's values and ethics. For Jews today, this same way of looking at life permeates everyday experience. A day opens with prayers to remind one of what is good, to see one's blessings. Daily life offers one opportunities to be a blessing for others in one's work and relationships. Such acts of kindness are not arbitrary or capricious, for they are part of God's own plan.

All of these ideals do not live merely in books or in teachings. They are visible, daily and concretely, in the vibrant communities of Jews who mark time by the Jewish calendar. Every Shabbat, the community comes together to read the torah, to pray, to eat a meal together, to enjoy each other's company, and to see their children play together. Sacred times and seasons throughout the year infuse a consciousness of God and love for the community. Everyone has a chance for a fresh start to strive to be a better person at Rosh Hashanah and Yom Kippur. The holiday of Sukkot marks the Almighty's protective care, where everyone, whether wealthy or poor, eats, prays, and celebrates in a simple structure—a *sukkah*. People with the means and wherewithal for preparing meals and entertaining seek those with nowhere to go. Hanukkah lights up the winter doldrums with sparks of spiritual insight and with happy children. Purim sends a reminder that miracles can occur in any age, and Passover and Shavuot root the community back to Sinai, revisiting the defining moments of being a Jew: the exodus from Egypt and God's giving of the torah. Besides the religious calendar, all of life's joys and sorrows are guided by Jewish instruction and customs. Every baby's birth is welcomed by the community, as are every child's *bar* and *bat mitzvah* and every couple's wedding. Those gathered say "*mazel tov*" (congratulations; lit., good fortune) to one another and not only to the one feted—because each milestone is for all Israel. And in times of sorrow, a *minyan* is gathered to pray, and Jews from throughout the community are present to be with the mourners for *shiva*.

My observations, to be sure, portray an ideal. But for all their idealism, they are also real. As I look around my congregation, I find, every week, the enthusiastic students who hear the torah portion, failed business owners and unemployed people who find courage not to give up, and the Russian-Jewish immigrants who, although once exiled to Siberia, are now praying in Hebrew. Until a few years ago, I heard Holocaust survivors—who lived through every unimaginable horror—lead prayers at Shabbat services (they have now since died). I see both the healthy and accomplished as well as the chronically ill or beleaguered thank God, do a *mitzvah*, support their schools and children's camps, sign up for a class. I know person after person who will offer a meal, watch a child, reach out in friendship, counsel and support, extend a handkerchief, write a check. I witness the passion of the young adults, adventurous and committed, who prepare to make *aliyah*, becoming citizens of Israel under the Law of Return. And at the *sukkah* party, hundreds of Jews from throughout my state (Wisconsin) lift their glasses and say, "*l'chaim*,"—to life! The ideals of Sinai continue in the humble room called my *shul*, in the warmth of the Shabbat dinners with my family and friends, in the offices and classrooms of rabbis and teachers, in my daughters' (Leah and Hannah Ariella) vibrant Israeli apartment filled with Jewish immigrants from around the globe, and in the very way Jews see the world. The Talmud teaches that when God gave the torah at Mt. Sinai, a covenant was made with all Jews—those standing there and those yet to come, because all Jewish souls were present at the moment of revelation (Talmud, *Shavuot* 39a). For Jews whose souls were at Sinai, home can be a precious place indeed.[2]

Notes

1. Stephen C. Lerner, "Choosing Judaism: Issues Relating to Conversion," in Rela M. Geffen, ed., *Celebration and Renewal: Rites of Passage in Judaism* (Philadelphia and Jerusalem: The Jewish Publication Society, 1993) 74.

2. An earlier version of this conclusion appeared in Sharon Pace, "The Appeal of Orthodox Judaism," *Clio's Psyche: Understanding the "Why" of Culture, Current Events, History, and Society* (Special Issue on the Psychology of Anti-Semitism and Judeophilia) 17/3 (2010): 210–15. Used with permission.

Pronunciation Guide

This transliteration guide is designed for readers who are unfamiliar with academic Hebrew transliteration systems.

ch is pronounced as in (the German) Ba**ch**
ts is pronounced as in cu**ts**
oo as in bamb**oo**
oh as in **Oh,** fine, thank you
ei as in **Hei**mlich maneuver
ai as in bons**ai**
oo as in ig**loo**
ee as in br**ee**ch
ah as in savann**ah**
ey as in gr**ey**
i as in ch**i**p
e as in j**e**t

Chapter 1

"*tohu* and *bohu*"	**toh**-hoo and **boh**-hoo
shema	she-**mah**
Avraham Aveinu	**ahv**-rah-hahm Ah-**vee**-noo
mitzvot	mitz-**voht**
Mitzraim	mitz-**rah**-yeem
Shimon Bar Yochai	Shi-**mohn** bahr Yoh **chai**
sefirot	se-fee-**roht**
tzimtzum	tsim-**tsoom**
tikkun	ti-**koon**

Chapter 2

mashach	mah-**shahch**
mashiach	mah-**shee**-ach

gehinnom	ge-hee-**nohm**
olam Ha Ba	oh-**lahm**-hah-**bah**
Yehuda Ha-Nasi	Ye-hoo-**dah**-ha-nah-**see**
shechinah or	she-chee-**nah**
shekinah	

Chapter 3

Tanak	tah-nahch
halacha(h) or	
halakhah	hah-lah-**chah**
agaddah	ah-gah-**dah**
peah	pe-**ah**
tzedakah	tze-dah-**kah**
Shulchan Aruch	shool-c**hahn**-ah-**rooch**
mezuzah	me-zoo-**zah**
kiddush	kee-**doosh**
tefillin	te-**fil**-in
tefillah	te-fee-**lah**

Chapter 4

Ashkenazim	Ash-ke-nah-**zeem**
Sephardim	Se-fahr-**deem**
berakhah	be-rah-**chah**
shema	she-**mah**
shemone esrei	she moh-ne **es**-rey
amidah	ah-**mee**-dah
bris/berit millah	bris/beh-**reet** mee-**lah**
ketubah	ke-**too**-bah
chuppah	choo-**pah** or **chuh**-pah
gan eden	gahn **ey**-den
shiva	**shih**-vah
kaddish	**kah**-dish
yahrzeit	**yahr**-zeit
tallit	tah-**leet**
tallis	**tah**-lis
tallit gadol	tah-**leet** gah-**dohl**
tallit katan	tah-**leet** kah-**tahn**
tzitzit	**tseet** tseet

minyan	*min-**yan*** or ***min**-yin*
yarmulke	**yah**-muh-kah
kippah	kee-**pah**
bimah	*bee-**mah***
chamsa	***chahm**-sah*
chai	*chai*
magen David	*mah-**gen** Dah-**veed***
l'chaim	*le **chai**-yeem*
sidra	*sid-**rah***
parsha	*pahr-**shah***
kashrut	*kash-**root***
pareve	***pahr**-ev*
terefah	*te-rey-**fah***
shochet	***shoh**-chet*
shemitah	she-**mee**-tah
rebbe	**re**-be
siddur	*see-**door***

Chapter 5

shavat	*shah-**vaht***
shabbat	*shah-**baht***
ger	*geyr*
minchah	*min-**chah***
kabbalat Shabbat	*kah-bah-**laht** shah-**baht***
maariv	*mah-ah-**reev***
lechah Dodi	*le-**chah** doh-**dee***
challahs	***chah**-lahs*
birkat hamazon	*beer-**kaht** hah-mah-**zohn***
devar torah	*de-**vahr** toh-**rah***
haftarah	*hahf-tah-**rah***
eruv	***ey**-roov*
havdalah	*hahv-dah-**lah***
Eliyahu ha Navi	*e-lee-**yah**-hoo ha-nah-**vee***

Chapter 6

Rosh Hashanah	rohsh-hah-shah-**nah**
Kol Nidrei	*kohl-**nid**-rey*
viduy	*vi-**doo**-ee*

lulav	loo-***lahv***
etrog	e-***trohg***
Shemini Atzeret	she-**min**-ee ahts-**e**-ret
Simchat Torah	sim-**chat** toh-**rah**
Hanukkah	chah-noo-**kah**
Tu B'Shevat	too be-**shvaht**
Seder	**sey**-der
Purim	poo-**reem**
Pur	*poor*
Megillah	*me-gee-**lah***
Hamantashen	***chah***-*men-tahsh-en*
Pesach	**pe**-sach
Hagaddah	Hah-gah-**dah**
matzah	*mah-**tsah***
Omer	**oh**-mer
Lag B'Omer	lahg be-**oh**-mer
Shavuot	shah-voo-**oht**
Tisha B'Av (The Ninth of Av)	tee-**shah** be'**ahv**
Yochanan ben Zakkai	**yoh**-chah-nahn ben zah-**kai**
Yavneh	**Yahv**-neh

Chapter 7

HaTikvah	*hah tik**vah***
Kinneret	kee-**ney**-ret
Shoah	*shoh-**ah***
Aliyah	*ah-lee-**yah***
Yom HaShoah	*yohm ha-shoh-**ah***
Yom Hazikaron	*yohm ha-zeek-ah-**rohn***
Yom HaAtzmaut	*yohm ha-ahts-mah-**oot***
Yom Yerushalayim	*yohm ye-roo-shah-**lah**-yim*
Yad Vashem	yahd vah-**shem**
ahavat Yisrael	*ah-hah-**vaht** yis-rah-**eyl***
Tsahal	***Tsa**-hahl*

Other available titles from SMYTH& HELWYS.

Beyond the American Dream
Millard Fuller

In 1968, Millard finished the story of his journey from pauper to millionaire to home builder. His wife, Linda, occasionally would ask him about getting it published, but Millard would reply, "Not now. I'm too busy." This is that story.   978-1-57312-563-5 272 pages/pb **$20.00**

The Black Church
Relevant or Irrelevant in the 21st Century?
Reginald F. Davis

The Black Church contends that a relevant church struggles to correct oppression, not maintain it. How can the black church focus on the liberation of the black community, thereby reclaiming the loyalty and respect of the black community?   978-1-57312-557-4 144 pages/pb **$15.00**

Blissful Affliction
The Ministry and Misery of Writing
Judson Edwards

Edwards draws from more than forty years of writing experience to explore why we use the written word to change lives and how to improve the writing craft.   978-1-57312-594-9 144 pages/pb **$15.00**

Bottom Line Beliefs
Twelve Doctrines All Christians Hold in Common (Sort of)
Michael B. Brown

Despite our differences, there are principles that are bedrock to the Christian faith. These are the subject of Michael Brown's *Bottom Line Beliefs*.   978-1-57312-520-8 112 pages/pb **$15.00**

Christian Civility in an Uncivil World
Mitch Carnell, ed.

When we encounter a Christian who thinks and believes differently, we often experience that difference as an attack on the principles upon which we have built our lives and as a betrayal to the faith. However, it is possible for Christians to retain their differences and yet unite in respect for each other. It is possible to love one another and at the same time retain our individual beliefs.

978-1-57312-537-6 160 pages/pb **$17.00**

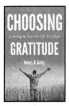

Choosing Gratitude
Learning to Love the Life You Have

James A. Autry

Autry reminds us that gratitude is a choice, a spiritual—not social—process. He suggests that if we cultivate gratitude as a way of being, we may not change the world and its ills, but we can change our response to the world. If we fill our lives with moments of gratitude, we will indeed love the life we have.   978-1-57312-614-4 144 pages/pb **$15.00**

Contextualizing the Gospel
A Homiletic Commentary on 1 Corinthians

Brian L. Harbour

Harbour examines every part of Paul's letter, providing a rich resource for those who want to struggle with the difficult texts as well as the simple texts, who want to know how God's word—all of it—intersects with their lives today. 978-1-57312-589-5 240 pages/pb **$19.00**

Dance Lessons
Moving to the Beat of God's Heart

Jeanie Miley

Miley shares her joys and struggles a she learns to "dance" with the Spirit of the Living God.   978-1-57312-622-9 240 pages/pb **$19.00**

The Disturbing Galilean
Essays About Jesus

Malcolm Tolbert

In this captivating collection of essays, Dr. Malcolm Tolbert reflects on nearly two dozen stories taken largely from the Synoptic Gospels. Those stories range from Jesus' birth, temptation, teaching, anguish at Gethsemane, and crucifixion.   978-1-57312-530-7 140 pages/pb **$15.00**

Divorce Ministry
A Guidebook

Charles Qualls

This book shares with the reader the value of establishing a divorce recovery ministry while also offering practical insights on establishing your own unique church-affiliated program. Whether you are working individually with one divorced person or leading a large group, *Divorce Ministry: A Guidebook* provides helpful resources to guide you through the emotional and relational issues divorced people often encounter.

978-1-57312-588-8 156 pages/pb **$16.00**

The Enoch Factor
The Sacred Art of Knowing God
Stephen McSwain

The Enoch Factor is a persuasive argument for a more enlightened religious dialogue in America, one that affirms the goals of all religions—guiding followers in self-awareness, finding serenity and happiness, and discovering what the author describes as "the sacred art of knowing God." *978-1-57312-556-7 256 pages/pb* **$21.00**

Faith Postures
Cultivating Christian Mindfulness
Holly Sprink

Sprink guides readers through her own growing awareness of God's desire for relationship and of developing the emotional, physical, spiritual postures that enable us to learn to be still, to listen, to be mindful of the One outside ourselves. *1-978-57312-547-5 160 pages/pb* **$16.00**

The Good News According to Jesus
A New Kind of Christianity for a New Kind of Christian
Chuck Queen

In *The Good News According to Jesus*, Chuck Queen contends that when we broaden our study of Jesus, the result is a richer, deeper, healthier, more relevant and holistic gospel, a Christianity that can transform this world into God's new world.

978-1-57312-528-4 216 pages/pb **$18.00**

Healing Our Hurts
Coping with Difficult Emotions
Daniel Bagby

In *Healing Our Hurts*, Daniel Bagby identifies and explains all the dynamics at play in these complex emotions. Offering practical biblical insights to these feelings, he interprets faith-based responses to separate overly religious piety from true, natural human emotion. This book helps us learn how to deal with life's difficult emotions in a redemptive and responsible way. *978-1-57312-613-7 144 pages/pb* **$15.00**

Hope for the Thinking Christian
Seeking a Path of Faith through Everyday Life
Stephen Reese

Readers who want to confront their faith more directly, to think it through and be open to God in an individual, authentic, spiritual encounter will find a resonant voice in Stephen Reese.

978-1-57312-553-6 160 pages/pb **$16.00**

Hoping Liberia
Stories of Civil War from Africa's First Republic
John Michael Helms

Through historical narrative, theological ponderings, personal confession, and thoughtful questions, Helms immerses readers into a period of political turmoil and violence, a devastating civil war, and the immeasurable suffering experienced by the Liberian people.

978-1-57312-544-4 208 pages/pb **$18.00**

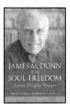

James (Smyth & Helwys Annual Bible Study series)
Being Right in a Wrong World
Michael D. McCullar

Unlike Paul, who wrote primarily to congregations defined by Gentile believers, James wrote to a dispersed and persecuted fellowship of Hebrew Christians who would soon endure even more difficulty in the coming years.

Teaching Guide 1-57312-604-5 160 pages/pb **$14.00**
Study Guide 1-57312-605-2 96 pages/pb **$6.00**

James M. Dunn and Soul Freedom
Aaron Douglas Weaver

James Milton Dunn, over the last fifty years, has been the most aggressive Baptist proponent for religious liberty in the United States. Soul freedom—voluntary uncoerced faith and an unfettered individual conscience before God—is the basis of his understanding of church-state separation and the historic Baptist basis of religious liberty.

978-1-57312-590-1 224 pages/pb **$18.00**

The Jesus Tribe
Following Christ in the Land of the Empire
Ronnie McBrayer

The Jesus Tribe fleshes out the implications, possibilities, contradictions, and complexities of what it means to live within the Jesus Tribe and in the shadow of the American Empire.

978-1-57312-592-5 208 pages/pb **$17.00**

Joint Venture
Jeanie Miley

Joint Venture is a memoir of the author's journey to find and express her inner, authentic self, not as an egotistical venture, but as a sacred responsibility and partnership with God. Miley's quest for Christian wholeness is a rich resource for other seekers.

978-1-57312-561-9 224 pages/pb **$17.00**

To order call **1-800-747-3016** or visit **www.helwys.com**

Let Me More of Their Beauty See
Reading Familiar Verses in Context
Diane G. Chen

Let Me More of Their Beauty See offers eight examples of how attention to the historical and literary settings can safeguard against taking a text out of context, bring out its transforming power in greater dimension, and help us apply Scripture appropriately in our daily lives.

978-1-57312-564-2 160 pages/pb **$17.00**

Looking Around for God
The Strangely Reverent Observations of an Unconventional Christian
James A. Autry

Looking Around for God, Autry's tenth book, is in many ways his most personal. In it he considers his unique life of faith and belief in God. Autry is a former Fortune 500 executive, author, poet, and consultant whose work has had a significant influence on leadership thinking.

978-157312-484-3 144 pages/pb **$16.00**

Maggie Lee for Good
Jinny and John Hinson

Maggie Lee for Good captures the essence of a young girl's boundless faith and spirit. Her parents' moving story of the accident that took her life will inspire readers who are facing loss, looking for evidence of God's sustaining grace, or searching for ways to make a meaningful difference in the lives of others.

978-1-57312-630-4 144 pages/pb **$15.00**

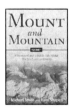

Mount and Mountain
Vol. 1: A Reverend and a Rabbi Talk About the Ten Commandments
Rami Shapiro and Michael Smith

Mount and Mountain represents the first half of an interfaith dialogue—a dialogue that neither preaches nor placates but challenges its participants to work both singly and together in the task of reinterpreting sacred texts. Mike and Rami discuss the nature of divinity, the power of faith, the beauty of myth and story, the necessity of doubt, the achievements, failings, and future of religion, and, above all, the struggle to live ethically and in harmony with the way of God.

978-1-57312-612-0 144 pages/pb **$15.00**

Overcoming Adolescence
Growing Beyond Childhood into Maturity
Marion D. Aldridge

In *Overcoming Adolescence*, Marion Aldridge poses questions for adults of all ages to consider. His challenge to readers is one he has personally worked to confront: to grow up *all the way*—mentally, physically, academically, socially, emotionally, and spiritually. The key not only involves knowing how to work through the process, but how to recognize what may be contributing to our perpetual adolescence.

978-1-57312-577-2 156 pages/pb **$17.00**

Psychic Pancakes & Communion Pizza
More Musings and Mutterings of a Church Misfit
Bert Montgomery

Psychic Pancakes & Communion Pizza is Bert Montgomery's highly anticipated follow-up to *Elvis, Willie, Jesus & Me* and contains further reflections on music, film, culture, life, and finding Jesus in the midst of it all. *978-1-57312-578-9 160 pages/pb* **$16.00**

Reading Job (Reading the Old Testament series)
A Literary and Theological Commentary
James L. Crenshaw

At issue in the Book of Job is a question with which most all of us struggle at some point in life, "Why do bad things happen to good people?" James Crenshaw has devoted his life to studying the disturbing matter of theodicy—divine justice—that troubles many people of faith.

978-1-57312-574-1 192 pages/pb **$22.00**

Reading Samuel (Reading the Old Testament series)
A Literary and Theological Commentary
Johanna W. H. van Wijk-Bos

Interpreted masterfully by preeminent Old Testament scholar Johanna W. H. van Wijk-Bos, the story of Samuel touches on a vast array of subjects that make up the rich fabric of human life. The reader gains an inside look at leadership, royal intrigue, military campaigns, occult practices, and the significance of religious objects of veneration.

978-1-57312-607-6 272 pages/pb **$22.00**

The Role of the Minister in a Dying Congregation
Lynwood B. Jenkins

In *The Role of the Minister in a Dying Congregation* Jenkins provides a courageous and responsible resource on one of the most critical issues in congregational life: how to help a congregation conclude its ministry life cycle with dignity and meaning.

978-1-57312-571-0 96 pages/pb **$14.00**

Sessions with Philippians (Session Bible Studies series)
Finding Joy in Community
Bo Prosser

In this brief letter to the Philippians, Paul makes clear the centrality of his faith in Jesus Christ, his love for the Philippian church, and his joy in serving both Christ and their church.

978-1-57312-579-6 112 pages/pb **$13.00**

Sessions with Samuel (Session Bible Studies series)
Stories from the Edge
Tony W. Cartledge

In these stories, Israel faces one crisis after another, a people constantly on the edge. Individuals like Saul and David find themselves on the edge as well, facing troubles of leadership and personal struggle. Yet, each crisis becomes a gateway for learning that God is always present, that hope remains.

978-1-57312-555-0 112 pages/pb **$13.00**

Silver Linings
My Life Before and After Challenger 7
June Scobee Rodgers

We know the public story of *Challenger 7*'s tragic destruction. That day, June's life took a new direction that ultimately led to the creation of the Challenger Center and to new life and new love. Her story of Christian faith and triumph over adversity will inspire readers of every age.

978-1-57312-570-3 352 pages/hc **$28.00**

Telling the Story
The Gospel in a Technological Age
J. Stanley Hargraves

From the advent of the printing press to modern church buildings with LCD projectors and computers, the church has adapted the means of communicating the gospel. Adapting that message to the available technology helps the church reach out in meaningful ways to people around the world.

978-1-57312-550-5 112 pages/pb **$14.00**

This is What a Preacher Looks Like
Sermons by Baptist Women in Ministry
Pamela Durso, ed.

A collection of sermons by thirty-six Baptist women, their voices are soft and loud, prophetic and pastoral, humorous and sincere. They are African American, Asian, Latina, and Caucasian. They are sisters, wives, mothers, grandmothers, aunts, and friends.

978-1-57312-554-3 144 pages/pb **$18.00**

To Be a Good and Faithful Servant
The Life and Work of a Minister
Cecil Sherman

This book offers a window into how one pastor navigated the many daily challenges and opportunities of ministerial life and shares that wisdom with church leaders wherever they are in life—whether serving as lay leaders or as ministers just out of seminary, midway through a career, or seeking renewal after many years of service. *978-1-57312-559-8 208 pages/pb* **$20.00**

Transformational Leadership
Leading with Integrity
Charles B. Bugg

"Transformational" leadership involves understanding and growing so that we can help create positive change in the world. This book encourages leaders to be willing to change if *they* want to help transform the world. They are honest about their personal strengths and weaknesses, and are not afraid of doing a fearless moral inventory of themselves.

978-1-57312-558-1 112 pages/pb **$14.00**

Written on My Heart
Daily Devotions for Your Journey through the Bible
Ann H. Smith

Smith takes readers on a fresh and exciting journey of daily readings of the Bible that will change, surprise, and renew you.

978-1-57312-549-9 288 pages/pb **$18.00**

When Crisis Comes Home
Revised and Expanded
John Lepper

The Bible is full of examples of how God's people, with homes grounded in the faith, faced crisis after crisis. These biblical personalities and families were not hopeless in the face of catastrophe— instead, their faith in God buoyed them, giving them hope for the future and strength to cope in the present. John Lepper will help you and your family prepare for, deal with, and learn from crises in your home. *978-1-57312-539-0 152 pages/pb* **$17.00**

Cecil Sherman Formations Commentary

Add the wit and wisdom of Cecil Sherman to your library. After 15 years of writing the Smyth & Helwys Formations Commentary, you can now purchase the 5-volume compilation covering the best of Cecil Sherman from Genesis to Revelation.

Vol. 1: Genesis–Job	*1-57312-476-1 208 pages/pb* **$17.00**
Vol. 2: Psalms–Malachi	*1-57312-477-X 208 pages/pb* **$17.00**
Vol. 3: Matthew–Mark	*1-57312-478-8 208 pages/pb* **$17.00**
Vol. 4: Luke–Acts	*1-57312-479-6 208 pages/pb* **$17.00**
Vol. 5: Romans–Revelation	*1-57312-480-X 208 pages/pb* **$17.00**